THE ANCIENT SPANIARDS

SAXON HOUSE

The Ancient
Spaniards

Gérard Nicolini

Translated by
Jean Stewart

SAXON HOUSE
D. C. Heath Ltd., Westmead, Farnborough, Hants, England

© 1973 Librairie Arthème Fayard. First published in French as *Les Ibère*

© 1974 Translation. D. C. Heath Ltd

ISBN 0 347 0023

Library of Congress Catalog Card Number 74-934

Printed in Great Britain by The Garden City Press Limited
Letchworth, Hertfordshire SG6 1JS

Designed by Peggy and Drummond Chapman

CONTENTS

List of Illustrations

List of Illustrations

List of Plates

Foreword

The progress of archaeology in recent decades has been spectacular in both its techniques and the widening scope of its field of action. A century ago, the history of ancient art was limited to Greek art, its Oriental antecedents and its Roman sequel. Classical art reflected, as in a mirror, the aesthetic ideal of the educated public, which took as its criterion the sculpture and monuments of Greece. These were held to be unequalled, largely because they seemed to be on a human scale and to wear man's likeness.

Greek meant beautiful; whatever was not Greek was inevitably less beautiful. But it was chiefly because Greek artists, particularly sculptors, had achieved a faithful representation of man that their work was held to be the model *par excellence* for any artistic endeavour and the high point of aesthetic expression. If this point of view was open to question – for nothing could be further from reality than some Classical works – it had nevertheless a long history. Taste had scarcely evolved since the first century B.C., when Cicero declared a preference for one particular statue over another which seemed to him less faithful and lifelike as an image of man.

Thus Roman art-lovers and their contemporaries neglected archaic and 'barbarian' statues as being devoid of interest, and preferred those of the Classical and Hellenistic schools as being more 'real'. The outcome has been both disastrous and fortunate for us: it involved the loss, through purchase, removal, plunder and destruction, of many admirable Classical and post-Classical works, but at the same time many of the despised archaic and 'barbarian' works lay buried from early times and have thus been preserved.

Things have changed today. Since the advent of modern art, especially abstract art, taste has gradually altered, or rather it has been enriched. The inestimable value of archaic and primitive art has finally been discovered and we now realise that creation and invention were not the prerogative of Greek art alone. Roman art has been freed from the overwhelming domination of its predecessor. And lastly, we have come to see in their proper context the art of the 'peripherae'; that is, of the so-called barbarian peoples on the confines of the Oriental, Greek and Roman domains in Asia, Africa and Europe. In this way the art of the Etruscans, the Scythians, the Gauls, the Phoenicians and the Iberians, to name only a few, have been appreciated by the general public and then studied with ever-increasing thoroughness.

In 1963 the Eighth International Congress of Archaeology was held in Paris and its sessions were devoted to these 'peripheral' arts. From that date the art of the barbarians was accepted, taking its rightful place in the aesthetic canon of our day. Its individual characteristics are being recognised, as are its relations with Classical art. Meanwhile the art historian and the archaeologist are gradually abandoning those assessments of aesthetic value which are out of place in the field of scientific research, and the would-be hierarchy of the arts is collapsing.

Collectors nowadays tend to take a greater interest in primitive or 'barbaric' works than in those of the Classical or Hellenistic periods. The latter in particular appear to have been affected by the change in taste, sometimes most unfairly. Antique works of art are no longer judged by their representational qualities, and surprisingly this broadening of taste has also advanced our knowledge of the Classical arts themselves. It has helped us to understand their genesis in the first uncertain efforts of the archaic period and their disappearance during the closing days of the ancient world, when the arts of the 'barbarians', by a kind of retaliation, gradually altered their form and then their content.

Of all the 'barbarian' arts, Iberian art is probably the least well known to the general public. Few of the numerous travellers to Spain are aware of the incomparable archaeological wealth of ancient Iberia. Many would be amazed if they could be taken on organised tours, as in Greece or Italy, and shown the many Roman and even Greek monuments still excellently preserved; for instance, large-scale remains of pre-Roman Iberian architecture, hundreds of treasure-hoards quite as rich as those of the Etruscans, marble statues and bronze and terracotta statuettes even more numerous than those of Greece and Etruria put together.

It is high time, then, that the general public, whose interest is being stimulated today in so many ways, should become acquainted with the art of ancient Spain, and more particularly with that of pre-Roman Iberia, the most vigorous and spontaneous native expression of Iberian civilisation and the surest means of fathoming its still undisclosed secrets.

Acknowledgements

I wish to thank all who have helped me to produce this book. In Madrid, the late Antonio García y Bellido, Director of the Instituto Español de Arqueología; Professor Martín Almagro Basch, Director of the Museo Arqueológico Nacional, Martín Almagro Gorbea, María Josefa Almagro Gorbea, and Señora María Luz Navarro, Curators of the same museum, and the late Augusto Fernández de Avilés; Professor Helmut Schlunk, Honorary Director of the Deutsches Archäologisches Institut of Madrid, and Dr Hermanfrid Schubart; Professor François Chevalier, Director of the Casa de Velázquez; and the Board of the Instituto de Valencia de Don Juan. In Barcelona, Professor Eduardo Ripoll Perelló, Director of the Museo Arqueológico Provincial, and Sr San Martín. In Valencia, Sr Domingo Fletcher Valls, Director of the Servicio de Investigaciones Prehistóricas, Sr Enrique Plá Ballester and his colleagues in the local museum. At Alicante, Sr Enrique Llobregat, Curator of the Provincial Museum. At Murcia, Sr Rafael Jorge Aragoneses, Curator of the Museo Arqueológico Provincial. At Jaén, Sr José Navarrete, Curator of the Museo Arqueológico Provincial. At Elche, Sr Alejandro Ramos Folques. At Alcoy, Sr Vicente Pascual Pérez.

I should also like to thank the photographers E. Domínguez (Museo Arqueológico Nacional) and P. Witte (Deutsches Archäologisches Institut) and I am particularly grateful to my friend Pierre Bonnard, without whom I could never have taken many of these photographs; also to Nadine and Yvon Drochon for their kindness. Finally I want to thank my wife for all her affectionate help; she will recognise here many of the journeys we have made together.

The photographs are the author's except the following: Museo Arqueológico Nacional, Madrid (2, 7, 14, 34, 40, 45, 46, 49, 63, 71, 73, 74, 75, 77, 111, 117); Domínguez Ramos, Madrid (pl. V, VII); Deutsches Archäologisches Institut, Abteilung Madrid (1, 3, 10, 18, 24, 40, 42, 53, 54, 88, 96, 107, 109, 110, 112, 113, 114, 115); Trabajos Fotográficos Aéreos, Madrid (26, 27).

CHAPTER 1
Iberian remains in Spanish soil

From the Renaissance onwards, scholars in Spain (as elsewhere in Europe) sought the origins of their national history in the writings of antiquity. They studied ancient maps and probed the *mores* of the earliest inhabitants. In an age when history concerned itself mainly with relating political events, they tended to collect stories of the wars that had troubled the Peninsula from the Carthaginian domination until the establishment of the *Pax Romana*.

From the sixteenth to the eighteenth centuries, the history of ancient Spain was based on this literary tradition. Moreover, it was accepted in an uncritical spirit without reference to such archaeological monuments as were then known. Also, from the sixteenth century onwards, it was often viewed in a patriotic light, both by scholars and the common people, who, profoundly respectful of their country's past, considered it as an inseparable part of themselves. Thus Cervantes, in his *Numancia*, extols the courage of the Spaniards (we should call them Celtiberians) who, preferring death to slavery when their city was beleaguered, evoked the admiration of their 'fierce conqueror' Scipio. And the Duero, personified as a strong man (just as the rivers of antiquity had been portrayed as deities), is made to declare: 'What jealousy, what dread, beloved Spain, will you arouse in those many foreign nations whose blood shall stain your sword, while your banner flies triumphant.'

Thus the heroism of the Numancians provides the basis for Spain's future military glory.

Of even greater interest for us is the mention in sixteenth-century literature of certain famous monuments of ancient art, such as the stone bull at the entrance to the Salamanca bridge against which poor Lazarillo de Tormes hit his head so painfully, or the celebrated bulls of Guisando to which Lope de Vega refers in *El mejor maestro el tiempo*. Obviously neither Lope de Vega nor the author of *Lazarillo* had any notion of the true archaeological character of these objects, which were connected with a very ancient cult and are today attributed to Celtic art under Iberian influence (fig. 1). Nevertheless they had been (and still are) preserved with jealous care and belonged to a centuries-old tradition.

Furthermore, a whole series of legends were associated with them, some at least going back to the Middle Ages. They were thought to be boundary-marks commemorating Roman victories: in some cases they were used in trials, being thought to reveal the guilt of the accused by changing colour. Apart from appearances in the Spanish Classical theatre and in popular tradition, Iberian remains are often described, with varying degrees of accuracy, in the first important studies of Spanish monuments; for instance, the *Libro de las Grandezas y cosas memorables de España* of Pedro de Medina, which appeared in Seville in 1548, or the huge inventory of *Las antigüedades de las ciudades de España* by Ambrosio de Morales, published in 1575 by command of Philip II.

But they are more particularly mentioned by scholars in local histories or regional inventories. Thus the learned Catalan Pons de Icart, writing in 1572, describes the cyclopean wall of Tarragona as one of the *grandezas* of that city with such remarkable accuracy that his work is still in use today for dating and locating its different sections. In 1610, Suarez de Salazar completed the same task for Cadiz. A few years later Rodrigo Caro, the first great Spanish archaeologist, published a detailed description of the antiquities of Seville and its surrounding area, based on a critical study of ancient texts. These include the famous *Periplus* of Avienus, which even today is open to a number of varied interpretations to be discussed later.

Thus the knowledge of ancient history progressed rapidly in

1 Avila. Wild boar carved in stone

eighteenth-century Spain, in spite of hypotheses now admitted to be mistaken but which widened the scope of research in their day. For instance, in the case of pre-Roman monuments mentioned in these studies, the Reverend Father Miguel Pérez Pastor, who was interested in the god Endovellicus, mistook the bronze ex-votos of the Iberian period for Egyptian deities, whereas Canon Lozano, writing the history of Jumilla, a little town in the province of Murcia, identified them with Greek or Roman gods. However, not everything in the writings of this period is to be dismissed; Pérez Quintero, in 1790, raises the problem of the famous tin islands, the Cassiterides, which were located by some off the Cornish coast and by others to the west of Galicia, opposite Cape Finisterre. If he opted for the second theory, it was probably through archaeological patriotism.

In the nineteenth century research took a new turn. Selective catalogues attempted to classify antiquities according to their period. The best known of these is probably that of Ceán Bermúdez which appeared in 1832: *Sumario de las antigüedades que hay en España*. This interesting attempt sought to record Roman monuments at a time when the study of antiquity was much more advanced and had suggested the existence of civilisations before the Roman arrival in Spain. But it was not easy to distinguish between Roman and pre-Roman antiquities – even today it is still hard to do so in certain cases – and the author included in his *Sumario* a number of pre-Roman objects. In spite of the modest bulk of this unillustrated work, the result attained is surprising in view of the difficulties confronting a scholar of that time as regards travel, field-work and the examination of local collections. Ceán Bermúdez's book was followed by a series of methodical inventories such as the *Diccionario geogràphico–histórico* by Miguel Cortés y López (1835), devoted to the three Roman provinces of Tarragona, Betica and Lusitania.

Thus by about the middle of the nineteenth century, archaeological research had made considerable progress. It became customary at this time to distinguish between the historic period, dating from the arrival of the Romans in Spain, and the pre-historic period that preceded it. But scientific study of pre-history was to emerge only in the following decades.

A new era opened with the work of Emil Hübner. This German scholar, the first foreigner to interest himself in Spanish antiquities, drew up a catalogue of the antiquities in the collections of Madrid (1862) and then undertook a work on Spanish archaeology, perhaps the first historical synthesis to be made with the aid of pictorial and sculptural objects (1888). But Hübner did not always succeed in distinguishing strictly Iberian antiquities from those of the same period left by other peoples from neighbouring regions. The importance of his work lay in the new direction it gave to archaeological studies. Faced with the ever-increasing number of discoveries, at a time when major excavations had begun on Iberian sites, he recommended the systematic grouping of Iberian monuments without which, he said, any serious study would be impossible.

The start of systematic excavation

Until the later nineteenth century, Spanish archaeology was based chiefly on the study of familiar monuments above ground and of chance discoveries: ancient walls, items of furniture, carvings, jewellery and ceramics unearthed during cultivation of the land or public building. There was also some clandestine excavation, often by the owners of archaeological sites themselves. In all fairness, such excavation can scarcely be called clandestine, since no law as yet existed to organise archaeological prospecting.

About 1870 the situation changed. Although chance discoveries still added their quota, archaeological prospecting was now controlled by the State through a decree of the Ministry of Public Works. Selected areas of research were entrusted to experienced archaeologists, usually after a proper examination of the site, and most frequently as a result of chance discoveries. This was how the site of El Cerro de los Santos came to be excavated in 1871 by Paulín Savirón.

Iberian remains in
Spanish soil

Subsequently excavations increased in number and completely altered the data of the Iberian problem. An abundance of unearthed material now made possible numerous archaeological comparisons. Moreover, by comparing them with those existing in other countries, it became possible to establish the first chronological systems. Certain sites, more or less completely excavated, yielded enough material for monographs. The comparative study of sites, even before the 1914 war, enabled scholars to determine more clearly the regions inhabited by different peoples in ancient Spain and the zones of foreign influence.

But this policy of systematic excavation had its disadvantages. At the time, scientific digging was unknown. Some very able archaeologists neglected valuable evidence, now irreparably lost, which would have enabled them to determine more exactly the stratification and date of the objects discovered. Thus L. Maraver, Director of the museum of Cordoba, excavated the site of Almedinilla (Cordoba), but the superb weapons he found there, Iberian *falcatas*, were handed over to the Madrid museum with no indication of their exact derivation. On the site itself, no archaeological context was noted.

Investigations were universally conducted in this way, here as elsewhere, at this time (1867). People were concerned only to salvage the most valuable objects in the best possible condition, without paying much attention to their context. Such objects were indeed subjected to scientific investigation, but this formed a separate study, undertaken in the peace and quiet of the museum, away from the site. Furthermore, the archaeologists who explored and those who published were not always the same, which made things even more complex.

Following Hübner, a number of foreign scholars interested themselves in Spain. Among them were the brothers M. and L. Siret, mining engineers turned archaeologists. Despite some inaccuracies, they established the relations existing between the Mediterranean and Spain from the Bronze Age onwards through their excavations of sites in the Spanish Levant and later in Villaricos, the ancient Baria, where for the first time Phoenician objects were unearthed.

Iberian art suddenly won fame and attracted public attention with the chance discovery in 1897 of the Dama de Elche, which was immediately displayed in the Louvre, thanks to the efforts of Pierre Paris. A few years later this great French archaeologist introduced us to the pre-Roman art of Spain with his celebrated *Essai sur l'Art et l'Industrie de l'Espagne primitive*, which won him the Martorell Prize and was long to remain the most reliable catalogue of Iberian monuments, in spite of some considerable errors of judgement. Appointed Director of the Casa de Velázquez, the School of Advanced Hispanic Studies in Madrid, Pierre Paris went on to publish his once-famous, though now forgotten, *Promenades archéologiques*.

But it would be misleading to portray Pierre Paris as a scholar confined to his study among books and rare objects. He was also a dedicated field archaeologist, who excavated the Ibero-Roman stronghold of Osuna (Seville) with Arthur Engel in 1904 and later the Roman city of Belo, on the Straits of Gibraltar, with a team that included Georges Bonsor, the explorer of pre-Roman Andalusia.

While Pierre Paris was working on his essay, J. R. Melida, Director of the National Archaeological Museum at Madrid, was completing the immense task of listing and classifying the Iberian bronzes and stone statues from El Cerro de los Santos.

At the beginning of the present century, the leading German archaeologist in Spain was undoubtedly Adolf Schulten, who directed the excavation of Numancia, which he described in a monumental volume. His fertile mind led him occasionally to put forwarb erroneous hypotheses, notably about the occupation of the Meseta by Iberians, Basques and Ligurians. These none the less had the merit of broadening the field of research, as did his basic work on the problem of Tartessos and on the geography of the Peninsula in ancient times.

Side by side with Schulten's work we must set that of Juan

Cabré, a scholar whose many qualities included a concern for accuracy. A highly talented photographer and draughtsman, he produced an illustrated account of the Celtic weapons and ornaments of cemeteries in the Spanish interior, and prepared a relatively satisfactory chronology. He also published accounts of the sites of Despeñaperros and Castellar de Santisteban, in which Iberian bronzes had been found, collaborating in the latter case with Raymond Lantier. In this connection the French scholar corrected the mistakes in Pierre Paris's chronology. A few years later, he raised the question of the origins of Iberian sculpture.

The period of the First World War saw the creation of the *Junta superior de Excavaciones y Antigüedades*, which was to co-ordinate the efforts of archaeologists and publish systematic accounts of excavations, henceforward subject to State legislation. The department has since changed its name, but the same policy is being successfully carried out.

Modern archaeological prospecting and present-day problems

A department in charge of antiquities made possible the development of new and more reliable syntheses. We must mention among others the work of Pedro Bosch Gimpera, Director of the *Institut d'Estudis Catalans*, who, investigating Lower Aragon and Catalonia, established a chronology of Iberian finds and a classification of painted ceramics. Finally, he tackled the problem of Iberian origins. In his view, the Iberians of eastern and south-eastern Spain sprang from a fusion of two ethnic elements, Capsians and Ibero-Saharians from Africa, whereas the Iberians of the south constituted an indigenous branch originating from Lower Andalusia. At the same time he postulated two waves of Celtic influence, imposed by successive invasions at the end of the Bronze Age and in the first Iron Age.

The ideas put forward by Bosch Gimpera, who is at present professor in the University of Mexico, made a considerable sensation, and were soon subjected to fierce discussion in the light of fresh archaeological discoveries. Meanwhile, research was being pursued on the language of the Iberians, whose alphabet had been deciphered without too much difficulty thanks to the names inscribed on coins. Manuel Gómez Moreno, following Schulten, recognised that there were in fact two Iberian alphabets, one Tartessian and one strictly Iberian, both related to the Creto-Cypriot syllabary and to the archaic Greek alphabet (fig. 2). The Iberian language was thus seen to be of non-Indo-European origin, but it has not yet proved possible to understand it.

Questions of origin and of chronology were very much to the fore when the Civil War broke out. During the Second World War, when the Lady of Elche was restored to Spain, A. García y Bellido advanced a sensational theory as to the formation and chronology of Iberian art. Whereas Bosch Gimpera had postulated too early a date for the first specimens of native art, García y Bellido envisaged it as a branch of Roman provincial art, preceded by an Orientalising Tartessian art in Andalusia and a provincial Greek art in the Spanish Levant, much earlier than the appearance of Iberian or Ibero-Roman art. These ideas inevitably aroused controversy, but the author's tremendous efforts took research a long way forward.

At the present moment, Spanish archaeology is more alive than ever. Martín Almagro, who excavated the famous Graeco-Iberian trade post of Ampurias, has sought to determine the chronological limits and the various periods of Iberian art. E. Cuadrado contributed greatly to our knowledge of Iberian civilisation by his excavations of El Cigarralejo and his brilliant syntheses. D. Fletcher Valls explored the site of La Bastida. A specialist in Iberian painted ceramics, he is now in charge of the rich specimens in the Valencia museum. J. Maluguer has been encouraged by recent excavations to return to the Tartessian problem. These scholars and many others, young and old, are engaged in the publication of their latest, often momentous, discoveries.

Furthermore, foreigners, particularly Germans and Frenchmen, are taking an ever-increasing interest in Iberian history, and a valuable international collaboration has been established, thanks to the generous welcome afforded by Spanish scholars.

CHAPTER 2
Iberia in antiquity: a legendary Far West

The situation of Iberia according to ancient texts

The geographical concepts of the ancient world are hard for us to grasp today with any accuracy. The men of antiquity, to whom the concept of the world's roundness probably occurred quite early on (although that notion was not admitted by all), imagined the known world – the *oekoumene* – to be surrounded by the waters of the Ocean. These lands, divided into three continents, enclosed an inner sea – the Mediterranean – which constituted both a link between neighbours along its shores and a route towards the outer seas. But maritime exploration was for a long time limited to the eastern basin of the Mediterranean, and Iberia, to the west of the western basin, is not mentioned until quite late on in ancient texts.

It is in the Bible, in the first book of Kings, composed about 950 B.C., that Iberia is mentioned for the first time to our knowledge. Solomon and his friend Hiram, King of Tyre, are said to have armed a fleet – 'once in three years came the navy of Tarshish, bringing gold and silver, ivory, apes and peacocks' (I Kings 10). Later, in the eighth century, Isaiah foretells the ruin of Tyre by proclaiming, 'Howl, ye ships of Tarshish!' (Isaiah 23), and that 'those that escape' the Lord's wrath are to be sent to Tarshish to declare his glory among the Gentiles. It was for Tarshish that Jonah set sail to flee from the presence of the Lord; and Ezekiel, in the sixth century, refers to the 'silver, iron, tin and lead' traded in Tarshish (Ezekiel 27).

Iberia in antiquity: a legendary Far West

Tarshish must undoubtedly be identified with Tartessos, in southern Spain. But the Bible is strangely imprecise about the place. Is it a country or a town? We only know that it is somewhere remote, since the journey there and back from Tyre took three years. Here we are confronted with an archaeological and historical problem which has not yet been completely solved. The Biblical Tarshish reminds one of the 'Indies' of the sixteenth century, and one is tempted to see a parallel between the organisation of the 'ships of Tarshish' and that of the companies that traded then with distant lands. We shall return to this later.

The legendary character of southern Spain reappears in the myth of Herakles, which first enters written tradition in Hesiod's *Theogony* and subsequently acquired abundant elaborations. Three of the labours of Herakles took place in the Far West: the lifting of Geryon's cattle, the capture of Cerberus and the quest for the Golden Apples of the Hesperides. The first two of these exploits are unquestionably connected with Spain. Geryon reigned over the island of Erythia – identified by Schulten as the island of Tartessos – or even over the whole of Tartessos. To get there Herakles sailed in the golden goblet of the sun over the turbulent ocean, which he calmed by threatening it with his bow. On his return he erected pillars on either side of the Straits of Gibraltar, and sailed up along the eastern coast of Spain towards Liguria, by the route later called *via Heraclea* in memory of his adventure.

The concordance between myth and geography is obvious here. It is less so, indeed, in the story of Cerberus. The latter was sometimes considered as keeper, with the dog Orthros, of Geryon's cattle, and more often as guardian of the underworld. But since, according to Avienus, the entry to the underworld was situated in the Far West, it is tempting to envisage Spain as the scene of Herakles's capture of the monstrous animal.

There is greater uncertainty as regards the Golden Apples of the Hesperides. We must firmly set aside the fanciful legend that identifies the golden apples of the fable with oranges. As is well known, the Hesperides were nymphs, daughters of Night. Their garden was near Mount Atlas, but there is nothing to tell us that it was in the Peninsula. However, one of the Hesperides was named Erythia, like Geryon's island.

Although the Bible and mythology are vague as to the position of Iberia, including Tarshish-Tartessos, this is more clearly indicated in the great geographical works of antiquity. Unfortunately few of these are original; the authors copied one another, and some of their mistakes are not easy to unravel. Take the case of the famous Hecateus of Miletos. About 500 B.C. he wrote a work of considerable size, which has almost completely disappeared. Stephanus of Byzantium, compiling his geographical dictionary at the end of the fifth century A.D., quotes Hecateus's text a thousand years after the author's death. He refers to Tartessos as a confederation of cities, apparently confusing Iberians with Tartessians. Is his account really based on the text of Hecateus, or should it be considered as an extrapolation of his own?

A similar and equally tricky problem is posed by the famous poem of Avienus, *Ora Maritima*, which gives the most complete picture that we have of the coasts of ancient Spain. The author lived under Theodosius, at the end of the fourth century, but his work is a Latin version of a Massaliotic *periplus* written in Greek in the sixth century B.C. Avienus is doubtless faithful enough to the old text, but he is not always very precise. Consequently there have been many interpretations of his poem over the past fifty years. According to him, Tartessos was at once an empire, a river, an island and a city. The Tartessian empire extended from the Mediterranean regions – the Spanish Levant – to Portugal, and, according to Avienus, the Iberians lived between Guadiana and Río Tinto in the south, and between the Levant and the Rhône in the east. He mentions the Greek colonies of Mainaké and Hemeroskopeion, but not the Phoenician ones of Sexi and Abdera. However, Avienus provides a mass of useful information. He finally proves to us that the coasts of the Peninsula were known beyond the Straits, at least as far as the western Pyrenees, as early as the fifth century B.C.

We have lost the *periplus* of Pytheas of Marseilles, a famous traveller who went round the Peninsula in about 330 B.C., but a series of scholars over the centuries made compilations of his work, and these are sometimes very valuable, as is shown by the case of Polybius.

The Greek historian of Rome, who knew Spain well, wrote an original work in the second century B.C., rejecting, or unfamiliar with, the tradition of the *peripli* and the statements and measurements provided by Pytheas. As a result, he makes bad mistakes about the shape of the Peninsula, which, according to him, stretches from west to east, with the Pyrenees running from north to south along its eastern border. This error was to be repeated by others, notably by Strabo two centuries later. Although the greater part of Polybius's book on Spain is lost, we gather that he located the Iberians, to whom he ascribed a high level of culture, in the east and south. He was probably the first to give the name Iberia to the whole Peninsula.

With Strabo, who under Tiberius wrote seven geography books describing the ancient world, documentation becomes more substantial. This author had never visited Spain but he repeats earlier descriptions, from Pytheas to Posidonius (who had written more than half a century earlier and from whose work he borrows liberally). The interest of his third book, which is entirely devoted to the Peninsula, is that it introduces us for the first time to the country's interior. Strabo distinguishes between four regions, corresponding not to the administrative divisions of the Roman Empire but to ethnic variations: Turdetania, Lusitania, Iberia and the Islands. His Iberia extends from the Pillars of Hercules to the Pyrenees, but its borders with Turdetania – the land of the Turdetanians, whom one would like to identify with the Tartessians or men of Tarshish – and Lusitania, which extends south-eastward to the sea, are not at all clearly defined. Finally Strabo repeats Polybius's 'projection' with the Pyrenees running from north to south. However, he corrects Polybius by giving the Peninsula a more compact shape.

Despite inevitable errors over the shape and dimension of the mainland, due to a system of measurement based solely on the coast line – like that to be found later in the early navigators' maps – and to the absence, in this part of the world, of astronomical measurements such as were used the East, it is interesting to note a certain agreement between these ancient sources as to the situation of the Iberians. Whether or not they distinguish these from the Turdetanians and Tartessians in the south, most authors locate them in a coastal fringe and its hinterland, extending from the mouth of the Guadiana to Languedoc. In the plains, particularly in Andalusia and Lower Aragon, they were believed to live a long way inland. As we shall see, this view is largely corroborated by archaeology.

Iberia and the Iberians as described in ancient texts

An arresting aspect of these ancient writers is their persistence in describing Iberia as an Eldorado. One cannot help comparing their tales with those of the Conquistadors of the New World who described the newly discovered riches of Peru and Mexico – both natural and human – with a naïveté sometimes tinged with exaggeration. But what seems to us exaggerated in the tradition of antiquity is in fact easily explained. First, we must remember that the 'geographical' traveller, until the time of the Empire, knew chiefly the rich coastal regions, and confined himself to a few observations on the more arid inland regions, particularly the great plateaux of the Meseta, then populated by Celts.

Later, at the time of Livy or Strabo, when the centre of the country was better known, the harsh and mountainous character of Spain was generally recognised. A little later still, Pliny speaks of the dry, sterile mountains he has visited. These writers, however, tell of the manifold riches of the country, and there is reason for this. The Spanish interior was probably more fertile in ancient times than it is today; the climate must have been much more humid. Above all there were far fewer inhabitants there to enjoy its natural resources. Thus Betica (Andalusia) could be considered one of the granaries of the Empire, whereas now it is the part of Spain with the lowest standard of living.

In most writings we note a clear-cut division between the Tartessian region, which had become Turdetania by the third century B.C., and the rest of Iberia, a poorer and wilder country, not always distinguished from the central regions of Aragon and Catalonia. We shall see that this division persisted through the Roman period, emphasised, as Strabo says, by the fact that the Turdetanians had become Romanised to the point of forgetting their own language, whereas the Iberians of the east and north retained their barbarian customs.

The wealth of the Tartessian land, already noted in the Bible and in the *peripli*, is stressed by Herodotus, writing in the middle of the fifth century B.C. He describes the discovery by the Greeks of this fabulous country. The Samian Kolaios was sailing towards Egypt when, driven off course by the east wind, he crossed the Mediterranean from end to end, passed through the Pillars of Hercules and reached this still unexploited country. Here he took on a cargo so rich that with one-tenth of his profits he dedicated to Hera, in her temple at Samos, a *krater* decorated with griffins' heads, upheld by three kneeling bronze figures seven cubits high! We can imagine the value of this fantastic cargo, but we cannot believe in the chance or the ill wind that blew the Samian sailor off course.

Kolaios was no doubt deliberately following the route opened by Eastern sailors before him. But Herodotus provides an even more valuable piece of information in another passage, where the Phoceans meet the King of Tartessos, Arganthonios, whose name is symbolic – it might be translated 'covered with silver'. This king, famous for his philhellenism, was so rich and generous that he offered them the wherewithal to build a substantial wall around their good city of Phocea, which was threatened by the Persians. The rest of Herodotus's text contains few

Map of the Iberian Peninsula showing settlements of the early Spaniards

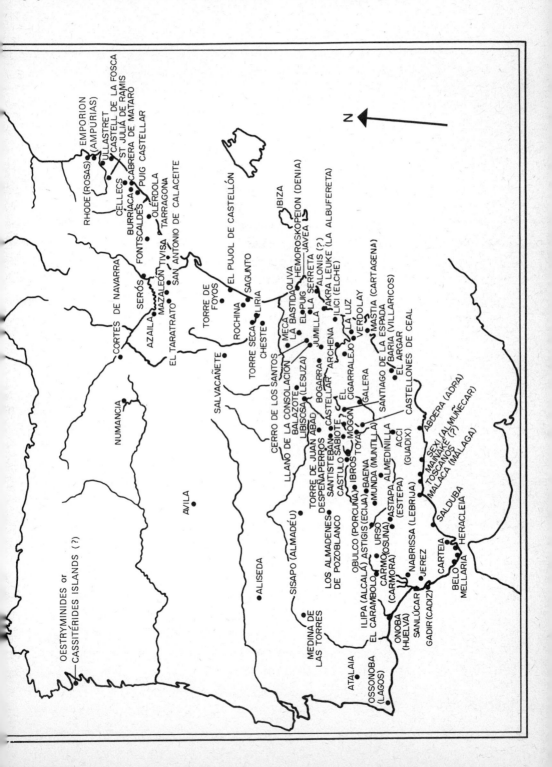

references to Iberia: he merely speaks (as does Aristophanes later) of Iberian mercenaries serving in Sicily.

Not much has come down to us of the work of Ephorus (later compiled by Timaeus and then by Strabo). Polybius is a valuable source of information. This Arcadian Greek, sent as a hostage to Rome in 168 B.C., undertook to write its history. He was primarily an eye-witness, who was with Scipio Aemilianus at the siege of Carthage in 146, and then during the Spanish wars and the capture of Numancia in 133. He travelled through Turdetania, the central region and the south-east. Of special interest are the first books of his *Histories*, relating the wars of Hannibal. Here he comments on the country and its inhabitants, especially the Turdetanians. Unfortunately we have lost almost the whole of books 34 and 35, which deal with the central and south-eastern parts of the country. These books were later compiled by Strabo and Appianus. A fuller picture was provided by the geography of Artemidorus, and in particular by the history of Posidonius, both writing in the first century B.C. Posidonius, another eye-witness, travelled all over Iberia, and described its geography, resources, inhabitants and their customs. Diodorus of Sicily, writing under Augustus, is one of the few authors to give information about the interior of Spain, probably following Timaeus and Posidonius. He also gives specific details about the Iberian mercenaries employed by the Carthaginians during the first Punic war.

His contemporary, Livy, chooses a more narrative approach to history. In books XXI to XLV, dealing with the second Punic war, we find facts related with admirable precision and striking details about the character of the Iberians, their devotion to causes and to persons, their unshakeable loyalty, heroism, cunning and savagery, which to some extent represent the typical 'barbarian' imagined by the Romans (in order to emphasise their own merits by contrast), but which are also real facts, as is the capture of Astapa, to which we shall refer later.

Strabo is our main source. At the time of Tiberius, he wrote a geography in Greek, the third book of which is devoted to Spain. He had never visited that country, yet he brings together and regroups with intelligence and a certain critical sense all the observations of Posidonius and Artemidorus and others from the lost books of Polybius, from the rhetorician Asclepiades of Myrlea, Timaeus and the various travel writers. Unfortunately his geographical division of Spain, mentioned earlier, sometimes makes it hard to attribute to any particular people or region the observations that he cites.

Thus we must be careful not to ascribe to the Iberians the characteristics of the inhabitants of the north-west or the centre. Indeed, Strabo applies the name Iberia to the whole of the Peninsula, as was common in his time. His geography is not free from glaring errors. In the introduction, he states that the north of Iberia is very cold (whereas we know the climate of Galicia to be the mildest in Spain) and that the south is fertile, especially beyond the Pillars of Hercules (which in fact was the case in his time). His division of Spain, as we have seen, was fanciful.

He begins with Turdetania and immediately praises its inhabitants as the most virtuous of the Iberians. He mentions the Celtici to the west, then the Bastetani to the south of the Betis (Guadalquivir), and follows the coast listing the cities. He speaks of the metal mines in the interior, but wrongly locates these in the north of the region. His inventory of the wealth of Turdetania is, however, fairly complete. He was the first geographer to have concerned himself with the problem of Tartessos, whose existence he questions, whether as city, river or region. He even goes so far as to criticise Homer's ideas on the far west. However, he is unable to give us any description of the *mores* of the Turdetanians before the Roman occupation.

Lusitania, which he considers next, extends (according to him) from the mouth of the Tagus to that vast realm of the Oretani which begins west of Castulo and reaches the sea of Alboran between the Bastuli and the Carpetani. Strabo was greatly interested in the Lusitanians, and he notes the savagery of their ways without however distinguishing between those of the east and those of the west. He goes on to describe the coastal region, from the Pillars of Hercules to the Pyrenees, recording the paucity of harbours before Tarragona, apart from the Phoenician colonies and New Carthage. He goes into particular detail about Emporion (Ampurias) and Rhode, but his account of the interior is vaguer. He describes the Campus Spartarius which lay to the south of Albacete, as a dependency of the town of Emporion, and puts the Oretani further north than he had previously done. He inserts at this point the geographical descriptions of Artemidorus, but since he has just been speaking of the land of the Vettones (now the region of Salamanca), it is doubtful whether these descriptions apply to the Iberians. He ends by describing the coastal islands, particularly Gadir, and offers his opinion about the Cassiterides.

Pomponius Mela, born in Cadiz about A.D. 25, had the great advantage of being a Spaniard, but his *Chorography*, describing Spain, is short-winded. Pliny the Elder is more eloquent in books III and IV of his *Natural History* (written about A.D. 70) in which he deals with the geography of Spain. He writes with less warmth than Strabo but gives more precise details. His book provides an extremely useful picture of the contours of the terrain, of the resources of the soil and subsoil, and of the different peoples that exploited these. We may profitably compare Pliny's observations with those of Ptolemy, a geographer of the second century A.D., particularly with regard to the specific location of the various Iberian nations. But the differences between the two texts pose certain problems. We must finally mention the historian Appian, a contemporary of Ptolemy's, to whose compilations we owe our knowledge of certain lost works, in particular the chapters of Polybius that deal with Spain.

The formation of Iberian civilisation

The texts of the aforementioned ancient writers cannot unfortunately give us any information about the origins of Iberian civilisation, which reaches back into pre-history. These origins must therefore be sought for in the soil of Spain.

Where did the Iberians come from? Historians such as L. Philippon, P. Bosch Gimpera, Blas Taracena and J. Caro Baroja have submitted theories as to the origin of the Iberians – African, autochthonous, European or Mediterranean – without however reaching a wholly satisfactory conclusion. The Iberians cremated their dead; and so there are not enough skeletal remains to enable us to establish any valid comparisons. If we seek the key to the enigma in pictorial art, we find represented a large number of physical types in which it is not easy to distinguish between reality and the artist's fancy. We shall therefore make no attempt to deal with this anthropological problem, particularly since it might involve the reader in a dangerous confusion between race and civilisation, a confusion which is practically non-existent in history. Let us rather consider the Iberians as a human group distinguished by Iberian civilisation, which is a real historic fact, and which can be approached through the intermediary of the writings of antiquity and above all today by a vast amount of archaeological evidence.

The precursors

As we have seen, the area of Iberia as imagined by the writers of antiquity was only approximately accurate. In reality it extended from the mouth of the Guadiana to the Pyrenees, consisting of two great regions. The first, to the south of the Peninsula, was very large, corresponding roughly to the Andalusia of today. With the Guadalquivir forming a broad groove down its centre, it took in the Sierra Morena in the north, the Betic chain in the south and the Segura mountains in the east.

The second region was more homogeneous. Spreading over the plateaux of Albacete and Lower Aragon, it dwindled to a strip of barely a hundred kilometres in width in the Valencia district and in Catalonia.

Iberia in antiquity: a legendary Far West

Finally, traces of the Iberians are to be found beyond the French frontier as far as the Rhône, but they were certainly much less deeply rooted in Languedoc than in Spain. The mountains and plateaux of Iberia were very varied. The great plains of the interior contrasted with the lowly *huertas* of the coast, and every type of shoreline could be found there – the wide beaches of the Valencia plain, the marshy coasts round Cartagena and the mouths of the Guadalquivir, the steep cliffs of the Spanish Levant and of Catalonia, which offered numerous harbours behind promontories or tongues of sand.

Nevertheless, the proximity of the sea conferred a certain homogeneity on the land of the Iberians. The Mediterranean climate prevailed everywhere, varying according to the altitude and the distance from the coast. It was by sea that men came to bring civilisation from the East or from more advanced Mediterranean countries. They swarmed along the coast or penetrated inland through the great valleys, making contact with peoples who may have come from remote parts of Europe.

Thus old civilisations took root and developed in this country which, from the earliest days, had welcomed strangers. And it is not surprising to find that the limits of Iberian occupation in pre-history – from the Upper Palaeolithic age – correspond to a division, a no-man's-land, between the cultures of the interior and those of the coastal zones. In the Neolithic period (5000–2500 B.C.), the concentration of human population seems particularly marked in Catalonia, the Spanish Levant and the Andalusian coastal region. We must imagine the cultures of this age as already marked by Oriental influence; one can trace the spread of 'cardial' pottery (decorated with the edge of a shell, the *cardium*) from Asia Minor to the Spanish Levant, by way of the northern and southern coasts of the Mediterranean. Certain anthropologists even believe that the nucleus of the Iberian people was formed during this period, deriving from a Mediterranean ethnic group serving as a link with the East. We may add that in the fourth millennium B.C.

*2 El Pujol de Castellón (Castellón). Lead
tablet inscribed with Levantine-Iberian script.*
(National Archaeological Museum,
Madrid)

collective tombs were already being built, inspired by those in
Anatolia and Palestine.

In the third millennium, at the beginning of the Chalcolithic
or Copper Age, the people of Spain used their own copper ore,
which they probably sold to the men of the East. This increase
in trade gave rise, about 2500 B.C., to two cultural centres, one
in the south-west of Portugal at Vila Nova de San Pedro, the
other in the province of Almeria, where the most famous site is
that of Los Millares. Here were built those remarkable collective
tombs with *tholoi*, round underground chambers reached by a
passage. Here too were made copper daggers with flanged blades.

Soon afterwards, in the same regions and in the interior of the
country, there grew up one of the centres of European bell-
beaker culture, characterised by bell-shaped bowls and cups, of a
type which was to prevail for a very long time. More indigenous
than the cultures that preceded it, it was dependent on the
Orient for its knowledge of metalworking. Although one cannot
truly speak of peninsular unity at this period, contacts between
the various human groups in the centre, south and east were
frequent.

Iberia in antiquity: a legendary Far West

Oriental influence persisted into the Bronze Age, when we still find a fairly sharp division between the cultures of the west (Portugal), south, south-east and north-east, the latter two being included in what was to be Iberia.

With Argaric culture (named after the village of El Argar in the north of the province of Almeria) in the middle Bronze Age, collective tombs were abandoned about 1700 B.C. and replaced by individual burials in cists – that is, rectangular stone coffins – or in jars with carinated bodies. In the heavily fortified sites of this culture, with their square-roomed houses, there have been found weapons and pottery which once again display the influence of the eastern Mediterranean. This brilliant culture formed one of the bases of Iberian civilisation which, a thousand years later, still retained certain of its features. But the Argaric culture was slow to spread inland. In the middle of the second millennium, Andalusia and the north-east were still going through a belated bell-beaker phase. Thus Catalonia in the eleventh century B.C. already had a markedly individual character, resting on a bell-beaker tradition and on various infusions from northern Italy, notably excised pottery.

The south-east was to preserve the techniques and shapes of El Argar until the eighth century – that is to say, practically until the birth of Iberian civilisation.

At the beginning of the first millennium new elements appeared which were to make possible the emergence of Ibero-Tartessian culture in the south and of new civilisations in the east and north-east.

In the ninth century a first wave of immigrants swept across Catalonia and Lower Aragon. These were representatives of the so-called urnfield culture, who were active farmers and were in the habit of cremating their dead. It has not yet been possible to establish a common origin between these peoples and the first Celtic invaders, who belonged to the European Hallstatt culture (Hallstatt B-C). In the eighth century there came a second wave of immigrants, akin in techniques to the people of northern Italy. Thanks to these new arrivals, Catalonia acquired in the sixth century a remarkable individuality, which enabled Iberian civilisation to develop in this region.

The Spanish Levant (the Mediterranean region) was scarcely affected by urnfield culture during the sixth century.

This seems to be true of Andalusia too, although seventh-century tombs of Celtic princes have been discovered in the upper and lower valleys of the Guadalquivir. Celtic influence has left little mark on this region, which retained an advanced form of Bronze Age techniques while adopting almost everywhere the principle of cremation.

The seventh century also witnessed the appearance of a phenomenon of fundamental importance, whose significance is even now not fully assessed: the introduction of iron working, which was seen for the first time in Aragon, in an urnfield site at Cortes de Navarra (Hallstatt C – about 650). It would seem probable that the use of iron was brought in from Europe by the Celts. But it is inconceivable that it should not also have been introduced through the Mediterranean, since by this time it had long been known by the peoples who traded with Spain.

The diversity of the regional cultures which were to serve as basis for the new civilisation can thus be perceived. Within these cultures themselves, ethnic groups reflect different origins due to successive invasions. Nevertheless, except in Catalonia, we must note the persistence of Bronze Age traditions and the scarcity of the Indo-European factor in Iberian territory.

The birth of Iberian civilisation and colonisation

Iberian civilisation was born from the encounter between these traditions and a new, powerful influence from the eastern Mediterranean due to intensified exchanges during the eighth and seventh centuries B.C. P. Demargne and E. Akurgal have analysed the debt of developing Greek art in the ninth and eighth centuries to the flourishing arts of the East. The same process took place in Iberia, although one cannot compare Greek and Iberian art in their early stages, the latter being much more independent because of the remoteness of Spain and its obviously less frequent contacts with outside influences. Nevertheless the phenomenon is part of a far wider movement which affected the arts of all Mediterranean countries. The hypothesis has even been put forward of an Orientalised community in the seventh century, dominating the shores of the Mediterranean and the arts of its peripherae. This is going too far, since at this period each art maintained and developed its individual character even while it came under Oriental influence.

How were contacts established? Trade exchanges have always played a significant part, but from the beginning of the first millennium onwards these were supplemented by the establishment of colonies along the coast. Here again the Phoenicians showed the way. As early as 1100 they founded Gadir, on the site of present-day Cadiz, almost simultaneously with Utica in Africa. Their object was unmistakable: to have an ocean port of call beyond the straits, on the old tin route, and to gain access to the metal wealth of Tarshish (Tartessos). The site was an admirable one and suited the Phoenicians. Like Tyre, it was an island situated some distance from the shore, which allowed it to be effectively defended and facilitated trade with the natives on the mainland. The Phoenicians of Gadir had no intention of settling in the interior of the country.

Starting from this position of strength, they were to set up other trade posts along the Mediterranean route. The oldest we know, dating from the end of the eighth century, is that of Toscanos-Torre del Mar (Málaga), whose ancient name is unknown. Excavations by the German Institute of Madrid have disclosed well constructed walls of rubble and unearthed an abundance of pottery, evidence of considerable activity.

From the seventh century onwards it becomes very hard to distinguish Phoenician from Carthaginian colonies. Immigrants from Carthage, which according to tradition was founded in 814, spread over the northern and southern coasts of the Sea of Alboran. It is possible that the foundation of Sexi (Almuñecar)

may have been due to Carthaginian enterprise; here the necropolis has yielded alabaster vases marked with the hieroglyphs
of ninth-century Pharaohs, which have obviously been re-used,
and a good deal of red-glazed Phoenician-Punic ceramic
ware. Of particular interest is the presence of two proto-
corinthian 'cotyles' or bowls, proving that right at the beginning
of the seventh century Eastern trade was already carrying
Greek objects. Other trade posts are possibly contemporary or
later: Malaca (Málaga), Abdera (Adra), Baria (Villaricos).

Somewhat later than Phoenicians and Carthaginians, at the
beginning of the eighth century perhaps, the Greeks also tried to
establish direct commercial relations with Tartessos or even with
the tin islands, sailing down the northern coast of the western
Mediterranean, the southern coast being firmly held by the
Phoenicians.

Rhodian and Samian ships brought various products, such as
pottery, bronze vases and weapons, which were redistributed
by the Phoenicians or the Tartessians, though it is not certain
how. It was towards the end of this first period of Greek trade
that Kolaios's voyage took place, and that Rhode (Rosas,
Gerona) was most probably founded. But the Greek ventures
never resulted in the setting-up of numerous colonies in Spain,
as they did in Italy at the same period.

The Phoceans were to alter the situation in the second half of
the seventh century. They attempted to establish a chain of
trade posts as far as Tartessos. Massalia (Marseilles) and
Emporion (Ampurias) were founded about 600 B.C. But
Mainaké (to the east of Málaga?) and Hemeroskopeion (Denia,
Alicante) were probably somewhat earlier, as was the problem-
atical Heracleia (Algeciras?). Alonis (Benidorm?) and Akra
Leuké (Alicante) were founded in the sixth and fifth centuries.

Mainaké was too advanced a post, and did not stand up long
against the hostility of Phoenicians and Carthaginians. In 540
the latter, in alliance with the Etruscans, won a naval victory
at Alalia (Aleria, Corsica) over the Phoceans, who had to abandon all hope of establishing themselves in southern Spain.

Punic influence predominated south of Cape de la Nao, and Carthage gained control of all trade in Tartessos, which does not imply that she refused to sell Greek objects to the Spaniards. But this Phocean withdrawal in the south promoted the rise of Massalia and Emporion. By 530 the inhabitants of the latter, feeling constricted in their old city, the Palaiopolis (San Martín de Ampurias), founded a great Nea Polis to the south on the other side of the harbour; many Greeks driven from home by events soon came to settle there.

In the fifth and fourth centuries, Carthaginian influence grew in the south, with Roman sanction. Akra Leuké however remained Greek throughout this period, if we are to trust the evidence of the material that has been unearthed; needless to say, this raises problems for archaeologists.

The third century ushered in a difficult period for Carthage. Rome broke the treaties she had concluded with the Carthaginians; during the first Punic war Carthage lost Sicily, then after peace had been signed, Corsica and Sardinia. Shortly afterwards she was torn apart by the wars of the mercenaries. Hamilcar Barca then decided to conquer Spain to provide Carthage with resources and restore her military strength, and above all to ensure his personal power. This marks a complete change in the history of Punic colonisation, which henceforward relied on political domination of an occupied country to exploit its economic and human resources.

Starting from Akra Leuké, which served as a base for his army, Hamilcar conquered Turdetania (Lower Andalusia). On his death, Hasdrubal made a virtually independent kingdom out of southern Spain. He founded Cartagena in 223 B.C., after settling the boundaries of the Carthaginian domain in Spain by a pact with Rome, the treaty of the Ebro. It was Hannibal's infringement of this treaty that set off the second Punic war, after which Spain passed under Roman domination.

CHAPTER 3
Iberian civilisation: the exploration of the land

To give a general sketch of Iberian civilisation presupposes – in addition to familiarity with the texts and the archaeological material – an adequate knowledge of the territory of present-day Spain. We shall not inflict on the reader, who can refer to modern writings on the subject, a geographical description of the mountain system of the Peninsula (as against the distribution of its elevations and depressions) or of the capricious behaviour of its rainfall resulting from that Mediterranean climate which prevails, to a greater or lesser degree, from the mouth of the Guadiana to that of the Rhône.

Today scholars seek the sites of Iberian or foreign settlements which have not yet been rediscovered, on the basis of the accounts in ancient writings of their former activities and of the rare vestiges which are found occasionally on the surface of the soil. Thus it has proved easy to locate, and to some extent to excavate, Almuñecar, Torre del Mar and Castulo. But one would like also to rediscover the places described by the writers of antiquity: Pliny's *Campus Spartarius*, south of Albacete, today a land of dry plateaux and extensively cultivated; the *mons Argentarius* of Avienus, the Sierra Morena with its rich mines of metal ore; to identify Calpe, the Fortunate Islands or the remote mysterious Cassiterides. The scholar, if he is not carried away by his dreams, will avoid the grave errors that arise from ascribing to a specific region an economic and consequently a social structure out of keeping with geographical factors. He will find that in Spain, probably more than elsewhere, these factors have shaped the history of the country's civilisation.

Iberian civilisation: the exploration of the land

Agriculture and animal husbandry

Undoubtedly an influential factor in the primitive landscape was the forest which clad most of the plateaux of Castile and of course the mountains of the Iberian region: the Sierra Nevada, the Segura and Celtiberian mountains and Upper Catalonia. The eastern Sierra Morena was known as the *Saltus Castulonensis – saltus* meaning a wooded grazing area. Strabo tells us that the mountain-dwellers of this region fed on acorn flour, and archaeology reveals their use of thick wooden beams as central supports in their dwellings and as a framework for the clay walls. While the Ebro Valley seems to have been an arid steppe, owing to its dry climate, the valley of the Guadalquivir (called Betis), the richest land in ancient Spain, also had its forests in the Atlantic coastal zone and in Upper Andalusia. The Turdetanians, according to Strabo, also used wood to build their ships. These forests certainly figured prominently in their lives. Furthermore they helped to conserve the soil by limiting the effects of water erosion and modified climatic conditions by bringing moisture and acting as windbreaks.

Besides timber, there were foodstuffs to be obtained from the forest. We learn, for example, of various species of fruit to be gathered there: figs, pomegranates (as one of the Liria paintings suggests) and also wild olives (which provided oil until the day the Iberians learned to graft them, possibly from Carthaginian experts). Leaves were widely used for litter. In fact the forests of Spain, like those of most countries in the ancient world, offered products which one would look for there in vain today, such as honey and wax, which were abundant and highly prized in Iberia. Honey was produced in Andalusia, where it was said to have been discovered by the Tartessian king Gargoris 'in the woods of Tartessos'. The Iberians used wax to model their statues. Strabo tells us that they also made vases of it in imitation of the Celts.

Hunting, too, was much practised in the forests, either on horseback or on foot, as we see from the Liria vases, the favourite quarry being stags, boars or wild pigs and particularly game birds. To this we must add the curious practice of rabbit hunting described by Strabo. It consisted of introducing into warrens those 'wild Libyan weasels' which were actually ferrets. This barbarous sport was naturally motivated by the abundance of rabbits and their destructive ways.

The Iberians' favourite sport was undoubtedly the capture of wild horses in the forests of the interior. These creatures, once tamed, were trained in the same way as the donkeys and mules which also grazed in the forest. According to E. Cuadrado, the horse was domesticated in Spain as early as the Bronze Age. The horses found in the interior of the Peninsula were very large (which perhaps partly accounts for their disproportionate size on the Liria vases), but the most highly prized were the small, swift, wiry horses of the north used for those mounted gymnastic exercises described by Strabo. Oxen and goats, valued for their flesh and their hides, were also bred in the wooded regions; some must still have been wild in the south-east to judge by the scenes depicted on the Liria vases. The pasture lands of Andalusia, whether wooded or not, even then fattened the bulls for which they are still famous today.

Finally sheep breeding must have become widespread on the high lands of the Meseta and in Turdetania, where its prosperity was such that a talent (26 kilos of silver) was paid for a breeding ram. As well as their wool, sheep provided the skins which were used as saddle blankets.

Clearly the forest was a source of considerable wealth for ancient Spain, in whose agricultural and pastoral economy it played a leading role. But whereas throughout the Iberian territory the method of exploiting forests was roughly uniform, agriculture varied markedly from one region to another.

The plain of the Guadalquivir (the Turdetania of antiquity) produced mainly cereals, especially wheat and barley, which were grown both in the dry areas and along the rivers, probably by spring sowing as is the case today. Andalusia was to form one of the granaries of Rome after the conquest.

The second source of wealth was oil, obtained no longer from wild olives but from trees grafted according to the technique introduced by the Phoenicians. Andalusia was the chief oil-producing region and probably, until the fourth century B.C., the only one.

The vine formed the third factor in this 'Mediterranean trilogy'. By the sixth century it was being cultivated throughout Betica, as far as southern Portugal. The wines of this region were the most famous in Spain.

Fruit-growing – grafted fig-trees, plum and apple-trees – was probably introduced in Andalusia by Phoenician or Carthaginian husbandmen. In the Roman period and probably earlier, there were irrigated gardens around certain towns where fruit-trees and vegetables were cultivated, including the famous artichokes of Cordoba.

The other regions of Iberia were not so rich. None the less the south-east and the Spanish Levant could already boast of their irrigated *huertas* where pomegranates, pear-trees, fig-trees and palms were grown. The *vega*, or cultivated plain of Segura, produced cereals. Olive-trees were common but vines seem to have been less widespread. Strabo also speaks of 'roots used for dyeing', which I have been unable to identify. Flax too must certainly have been cultivated in the lowlands of the Spanish Levant.

In the main, Aragon and Lower Catalonia cultivated cereals and to a lesser extent vines. Olives were not introduced until the fourth century, but then spread rapidly. Here, on the other hand, flax was in its element.

Artists have left few records of this agricultural wealth, about which we learn from ancient writers. But excavation has exposed agricultural tools of all sorts and these allow us to reconstitute the methods used for farming, at any rate in the Spanish Levant. A first group of implements was devoted to cereal farming (ploughshares, sowing-scoops, sickles and so on), whereas a second group served no doubt for the

gardening practised in irrigated zones and around settlements (garden forks, spades, hoes, adzes and dibbles).

Fishing and garum-making

On the vases found in Liria and the south-east and on certain
vessels from Tivisa, Iberian artists lay special emphasis on
symbols representing water and fishes. Indeed, many vessels
are abundantly decorated with fish. Fishing scenes however
are very rare, and it is uncertain whether as much importance
was attached to fishing before the Roman conquest as after it.

Classical authors (Eupolis, Antiphanes, Aristophanes) tell
us that the Iberians and the Gaditani fished, and that they
salted their catch, notably sturgeon and the muraena. Later
sources speak of mackerel and tunny and specify that the
great fishing region lay between Gadir and Cape de la Nao.
Fish passed regularly through this zone on their migrations
between the Atlantic and the Mediterranean, and salt-works
had naturally been set up there.

Even before the Romans came, the Iberians had certainly
begun to make their famous *garum* or *allec* (pickled fish),
which became during the Roman period one of the most
valued products of Turdetania and was exported throughout
the Mediterranean basin. This *garum* was made by soaking in
brine (*muria*) the viscera and blood of tunny fish, or else
whole mackerel. Successive decantations yielded a black
sauce which could be eaten by itself or as a condiment to
give flavour to insipid food. It was certainly a highly nutri-
tious product and could be used as a drink, mixed with water
or wine, or even as a medicine. Its adaptability naturally
added to its price.

Later, during the Roman period, methods of preparation
were constantly improved and diversified, the most famous
variety of pickle being the '*garum* of the allies', made from
whole mackerel. Trading posts for *garum* sprang up all along
the Spanish coast, notably at Lucentum (Tossal de Manises,
Alicante), Baria (Villaricos, Almeria), Sexi (Almuñecar,

Málaga), Salduba (San Pedro de Alcantara, Málaga),
Carteia (Algeciras, Cadiz), Mellaria and Belo. The Franco –
Spanish excavations at Casa de Velázquez since 1920
have revealed huge installations dating from the first and
third centuries B.C., including concrete salting vats that still
contained tunny fish skeletons.

Among the wealth derived from the sea, Strabo mentions
murex of exceptional size and the use of the purple dye extracted from this shellfish was doubtless introduced into
Spain by the Phoenicians or Carthaginians. He also refers
to oysters, cuttlefish and even whales found in the outer
sea.

The exploitation of the subsoil

Mining was as profitable as agriculture for those who practised it. In this respect the chief activity was the extraction
of copper ore of which Spain is still one of the world's richest
sources. The bulk of it was procured, then as now, from the
borders of the Sierra Morena, as well as from the Río Tinto
mines and those of Kotinai (possibly in the Linares region),
whose ore had a one-quarter metal content according to
Strabo. He speaks admiringly of the miners' skill in cutting
galleries and describes the Archimedean screws (which he
calls 'Egyptian spiral pumps') used to empty water from
underground rivers.

Next came lead and silver. These mines were situated
mostly in the regions of Castulo and Mastia (Cartagena). The
Castulo area had been christened the *mons Argentarius*.
During the Roman period silver mines were opened at
Acci (Guadix) and at Ilipa (Alcalá del Río, Seville). Strabo
once again praises the industry of the Turdetanian miners,
who could extract in three days the equivalent of one Eubean
talent (26 kilos of pure silver). In the Cartagena region there
have been discovered, among other tools, esparto baskets
with wooden frames and with a hook attached which served
to bring up the lead ore.

Gold was mainly extracted from rivers by washing in sluices, Roman specimens of which are still in existence. The Segura and all the rivers of the Sierra Nevada contained grains of gold dust of varying weights. The Iberians undoubtedly used some sort of wash-troughs, about which Strabo's text is inexplicit. Production here was considerable, though probably not on the scale of that in Galicia and the Asturias.

Iron ore, which had been extracted since the end of the eighth century, increased in output as a result of the need for weapons and tools. Iron came chiefly from Catalonia and Lower Aragon, a fact to which huge piles of iron dross along the Catalonian coast testify. Segura mines were probably already being worked in the Iberian period.

Metals were not the only products of the subsoil; it also yielded valuable dyes. For instance Iberian cinnabar (red mercuric sulphide) was mentioned by Theophrastus early in the third century B.C. We know from Pliny that minium (red lead) came from Sisapo (Almaden) and stocked the entire Roman market. The region still produces mercury. We may also mention the ochre (iron sulphide) found in the Murcia region, stibnite which supplied lubricants and black dye, and so forth.

Iberian industries

One always hesitates to speak of industry in the ancient world, whose techniques are more akin to crafts. The latter term, however, seems inadequate to characterise relatively large-scale production in certain fields, where as well as human labour (which was always preponderant) some fairly advanced machinery was used. This was the case with the Iberians' metallurgical industries in which complex mining equipment was employed.

Iron-working was predominant and produced weapons and tools. Weapons had been made since the Bronze Age in the Tartessian region, yet since the beginning of the Iron Age metallurgy had shifted towards the Sierra Morena and

the Meseta, the south-east, the Spanish Levant and Catalonia, where mineral ore was more abundant. Proximity to
forests was essential to secure a provision of charcoal.

Ancient writers praised the quality of Iberian work.
Towards the end of the third century B.C., Philo of Byzantium
informs us that Iberian swords were forged in the cold state
from pure soft iron. He adds that the smith tested them by
holding them above his head and bending them with both
hands till they touched his shoulder, and that they resumed their
original shape as soon as they were released! Diodorus adds
the curious information that they were buried in the earth
to purify the metal. In fact Iberian weapons were perhaps
better to look at than to fight with. The purity of the soft
iron, which made the blade easier to decorate, obviously
affected its hardness and resilience. Arribas has suggested that
Iberian swords were used chiefly for show.

Sites in the south-east and the Spanish Levant have again
furnished evidence of tool manufacture for all trades. Wood-
cutting axes, saws, wedges, gimlets, masons' trowels and
chisels, miners' and quarrymen's pickaxes, pincers, scissors
for sheep-shearing, needles for esparto stitching, jointed
compasses and engravers' tools (doubtless manufactured
for artists) have been found here.

Bronze-working was even more highly developed than
iron-working. The main centre was naturally the Tartessian
region because of the proximity of the copper mines. But we
know that tin had to be brought from the Cassiterides,
Galicia, or Cornwall in Britain. The bronze jugs and basins
discovered in the Tartessian region may perhaps have been
made in Lower Andalusia, at Gadir and Tartessos. The art
of metal-carving had developed mainly in the Sierra Morena.
Smelters' crucibles have come to light at Despeñaperros,
and the tools used for carving bronze statuettes have been
unearthed on other sites. But bronze was fashioned in other
ways – as pins, needles, razors, mirrors and above all the
fibulae or brooches, the production of which was widespread.

Leather and textile work

Leather is unfortunately a highly perishable material, and excavation seldom yields intact objects. Ox-hides from Turdetania and sheep-skins from the Sierra Morena and the south-east were used for clothing (headgear and shoes) and for saddlery, harness and belts. Moreover, the Lusitanians made small boats by stretching hides over a wooden frame.

Wool spinning and weaving was widespread, according to Strabo. From the black sheep of the Meseta and the Sierra Morena came the material for the Celtic *sagum* or mantle, but also probably for the cloaks and tunics of the Iberians, and the wool of the white sheep of Betica was used for Roman togas. Weaving may have been conducted on an appreciable scale at Saguntum or in the ports, but it was practised mainly as a cottage industry, as was the case throughout antiquity until the Roman period. This is made manifest by an abundance of loom-weights found in all excavated dwellings and sanctuaries.

Linen production, which was important, was devoted primarily to men's and women's lightweight garments. The weaving was done exclusively by women, as Ephorus tells us in the fourth century; they even competed for prizes.

The Iberians undoubtedly learned the art of linen weaving from the East. E. Cuadrado came across a large number of linen fragments in a Bronze Age necropolis, which implies that the use of linen in Spain goes back to the beginning of the second millennium. Other fragments have been unearthed from fourth-century tombs in the necropolis of El Cigarralejo.

Esparto may perhaps be ranked as a textile, since it was used in woven garments during the Bronze Age, although subsequently it was mainly used to make ropes, nets, mats and so forth. Esparto working was undoubtedly a widespread craft – until the coming of the Romans – over the whole of the *Campus Spartarius*; that is to say the region between

Albacete, Alicante and Almeria. Cartagena known as Spartaria, was the big export centre for this important industry, which reached its peak in the third century B.C.

Foreign and home trade

The historian seeking data on Iberian trade can consult the writings of Greeks or Romans, whose nations traded extensively with Iberia by sea. From these he will learn about foreign trade, more particularly about exports from Iberia. A knowledge of imports will have to depend, with a few exceptions, on the archaeologists' inventory of foreign products discovered in Spanish soil. But here any assessment of volume is a delicate matter, since statistics in archaeology are only relatively reliable.

As regards internal trade in the pre-Roman period, written evidence is scanty and here again we have to resort to archaeology for information. But this time the uncertainty is even greater, for too often the trade routes and all traces of exchange have been obliterated by the Roman occupation which, while pacifying the Peninsula, altered the movements of trade to a marked degree.

Foreign trade was characterised from the outset by what is known today as the colonial system. Spain's relation to the Mediterranean countries was that of a land producing raw materials bought by foreigners in exchange for valuable artifacts. Articles made in Iberia were exported through the medium of foreigners who were in charge of production and sale. The Tartessians formed the only exception to this general rule, since they traded on their own account with the north and with the Atlantic coastal regions and probably to some extent within the country itself.

To begin with, perhaps from the time of the foundation of Gadir in about 1100, the Phoenicians had complete control of trade and served as intermediaries between the far west and the eastern Mediterranean. They probably sailed up the coast of Africa. This was the period when the ships of

Tarshish set sail every three years. Tin was doubtless the prime object of this trade. We do not know if the Phoenicians themselves fetched it from the Cassiterides or whether the Tartessians acted as middlemen. Certainly the products of Andalusia, particularly its metals, were already being bought by Phoenicians, who sold Oriental and Greek products.

Increasing their commercial activity in the eighth and above all in the seventh centuries, they founded the trading posts of the Costa del Sol and the Moroccan coast (Mogador). At this time Tartessos gained its wealth and power by acting as middleman. A second period opened with the coming of the Greeks, Rhodians and then Samians, in the eighth century, who, after confronting the Phoenicians in the south, took the northern route along the coasts of Italy and Gaul. This trade was inconsiderable until the arrival of the Phoceans who, thanks to Massalia and Emporion, succeeded in trading as far as Cape de la Nao, but were unsuccessful in the south, where Phoenicians and Carthaginians were firmly established, the latter increasingly replacing the former.

With the victory of Alalia in 540 B.C. there began a third period, during which once again Carthage seized control of trade in spite of the restrictive treaties made with Rome and even in spite of the first Punic war (264–256). After this the foundation of the Barcid empire upset the political and economic state of southern and eastern Spain by attempting for the first time the direct exploitation of the country's agricultural, mining and industrial resources by foreigners, or rather for the benefit of their leader, Hamilcar Barca. But the Barcid empire had no chance to establish itself, for the second Punic war presently gave Spain more permanent masters – the Romans.

E. Cuadrado's interesting list of the products exported and imported reveals the disproportion between the two. Exports, consisting essentially of raw materials, included in the first place metals, of which gold and silver were naturally of prime importance. The metal trade was with the Mediterranean and the north.

Silver was exported through Lower Andalusia and through Mastia-Cartagena by Phoenicians and Carthaginians, together with Tartessians – Turdetanians; it was carried as far as the islands of the Cassiterides or the Oestrymnides, and there exchanged for tin which made up the return freight. The journey to the islands took about four months, according to Avienus, who relates the voyage of the Carthaginian Himilcon from Gadir along a route strewn with dangers. (The *periplus* no doubt exaggerates the horrors of the journey to discourage anyone from venturing to compete with the Carthaginians.)

Copper was also transported along the northern route, but an important quota was sent into the Mediterranean, especially after the exhaustion of Oriental deposits. The ore left Spain by way of Erbi-Onoba (Huelva), the city of Tartessos, or Gadir. But we know that the Tartessians also exported semi-processed products. In particular they alloyed copper and tin and sold the bronze both at home and abroad in the form of ingots. Lead and silver were probably transformed in the same way, either by the Tartessians or by foreign companies, as is suggested by the story of Timaeus, related by Diodorus: some merchants who could not take on all the silver they had bought replaced the lead in their anchors by silver.

At the time of the Romans, lead was exclusively exported in the form of ingots. However, the monopoly exercised by Rome over the transformation of cinnabar (which, according to Pliny, was forbidden in Spain) must certainly have had some precedents not only as regards minium, but also in respect of other metals and dyes based on metallic oxides (such as borax, used among other things for welding gold and copper carbonate).

After metals, slaves were probably the most profitable commodity for traders. The unfortunate prisoners taken by

Phoenicians and Greeks, and later by Carthaginians, during battles and raids were sold in all the Mediterranean markets and the African dominions of Carthage, where in fact they were treated with humanity.

The horses of Andalusia and the Spanish Levant and the mules of the Balearic islands proved a further source of wealth to both Carthaginians and Romans, who used them in their armies. The scale of their requirements is suggested by Polybius's inventory of Rome's military forces, made during the second Punic war, which included 37,000 cavalry. Spanish horses were also used for circuses, races and show-riding. Carthaginian merchants had a monopoly over the ropes, nets, pack-cloths and so forth made of esparto and used by the army and navy; they also exported the raw fibre.

There had already been a considerable trade in foodstuffs even before the Roman occupation. Carthage bought wheat and barley and resold them to the countries along the Mediterranean shores. The operation was profitable because of the absurdly low price of foodstuffs in Spain, on which Polybius comments. On the other hand the trade in honey and wax and also in *garum* (of which the Carthaginians definitely had a monopoly before the Romans came) must have been both ancient and lucrative, owing to the high value of these products relative to their weight. It has been possible to ascertain the routes followed by this trade by means of the containers found both on land and among the wreckage washed ashore. Punic amphorae, with their small handles and characteristically bulging bodies, were used to carry wine and oil; the pots used for *garum* and the alabaster vessels that contained colouring matter were naturally smaller. E. Cuadrado has suggested that honey was sold in Iberian *kalathoi*.

The question of exports is obviously connected with that of the diffusion of native ceramics, either used as containers or exported for their own sake. Thus Iberian pottery has been found at Oran, Ischia, Ventimiglia and Olbia (Hyères), dating from the fourth to the first centuries B.C.

Imports, in comparison, were likely to be valuable commodities, either raw materials or artifacts from more advanced Greek or Oriental countries.

Among the raw materials we must of course include tin, which was essential for founding bronze. But there were also amber, ivory, ostrich eggs (part of the equipment of tombs), and semi-precious stones used in the luxury industry of Tartessos. This industry produced articles copied from imported prototypes which have occasionally been unearthed.

The earliest manufactured articles imported included pieces of Greek armour, such as the famous helmet of Jerez, and Cypriot fibulae; these were brought to Spain by Greeks and Phoenicians, but never in considerable quantities. More copiously represented were the objects which we consider as true works of art, but which for the Greek and Oriental traders were probably mere makeweight stuff of no great value: statuettes and vases of alabaster or bronze, multi-coloured glass beads (sometimes as big as an egg), and scarabs by the thousand. But the bulk of these imports consisted of pottery from Cyprus, Phoenicia or Greece, especially after the middle of the fifth century, when red-figure vases from Athens were used on ceremonial occasions in the south-east and Catalonia. It was to be superseded, as we know, by Italic pottery. Who brought it to Spain? Undoubtedly the Carthaginians, in competition with the Massaliots and then with the Italians themselves.

Our knowledge of the methods of transaction is meagre, but these must have evolved substantially between the seventh and second centuries. It has often been supposed, following the accounts of Greek geographers, that goods were bartered directly on the shore while foreign merchants waited some distance away without making contact with the natives. This must have been true in some cases and explains why the Phoenicians settled in off-shore islands as at Gadir.

3 Ampurias (Gerona). Coins from the Iberian town of Indika, inscribed with the letters U-N-DI-CE-S-CE-N. Third or second century. (Archaeological Museum, Barcelona)

But in the Tartessian region as early as the seventh and sixth centuries, then in the Spanish Levant and Catalonia from the fifth century onwards, transactions grew more elaborate. Bartering certainly went on, particularly in the interior, but money was used increasingly. Greek and Phocean coins of the sixth century have been discovered, others from Rhodes, Magna Graecia and Marseilles and finally Carthaginian coins of the third century. Coins minted at Ampurias appeared in the fifth century, but it was chiefly from the third century onward that the Iberians took to imitating Greek coins, as we see in the specimens from Indika (fig. 3), which incidentally are found only in the coastal regions.

Internal trade depended greatly on foreign trade. Ever since the time of the first Phoenician merchants, routes had been developed to serve the purposes of large-scale commerce. The first of these was probably the coastal route which catered for local traffic, carrying salt from the south to the *garum*

44

installations and articles of esparto towards the south and the north-east, and ensuring the distribution of all imported products. We may picture these exchanges as taking place in two zones, on either side of Cape de la Nao, the south being the preserve of Tartessian sailors and the north, perhaps, of the Greeks. This coastal route, which was also favoured by foreign traders, is the one best known to us, thanks to the *peripli* written from the sixth century onwards and to the geographers who summarised or simplified these.

The *via Heraclea*, one of the earliest Iberian land routes, ran partly parallel with the sea route; from remote times it had linked Italy to the Spanish Levant, following the coast-line. At a later period, possibly under the Barcids, it was joined by the Guadalquivir road running from Gadir to Upper Andalusia. Two other roads connected Mainaké to the city of Tartessos and the mouth of the Guadiana to that of the Tagus. Other land routes ran from Andalusia to the Meseta region. The most important was that which went through Despeña-perros to La Mancha. Another, further west, led from the coast to the metal deposits of the Sierra Morena and must have continued towards Estremadura and western Castile, to judge by the distribution of Tartessian objects that have been discovered.

Along with these land routes there must obviously have been waterways. Strabo informs us that the Guadalquivir was navigable for light craft as far as Castulo. The Ebro, the Jucar and the Segura – which was a larger river at that time – must also have been navigable, at any rate in part.

All these routes by land or water proceeded to ports or followed the coast, and could thus be used to transport the raw materials purchased by foreigners. The cultural role which the latter came to play, albeit accidentally, was very important, since it was by their means, and along these routes, that the influences which generated and developed Iberian art spread into the interior of the country.

CHAPTER 4
Iberian civilisation: political and social structures

The political unity of Iberia was not achieved until the Romans dominated the country. A number of factors accounted for this: the country's division into regions between which there was little contact, the probable diversity of origin between the various tribes and the different Mediterranean influences which emphasised that disparity between ethnic groups which is revealed more particularly by the plurality of writing systems.

Nevertheless there were certain features of the Iberian character, to which we shall return later, which might have brought the people together around a leader: marked patriotism when confronting an enemy, the stubbornness with which they would fight to the death rather than surrender, the loyalty expressed by *devotio* ('sublimated friendship', as García y Bellido calls it) demanding an absolute identity of feeling and behaviour to the point of obligatory suicide on the death of the leader. But these traits, which did not escape the notice of ambitious men like Hamilcar Barca, were displayed only within limited political and social settings. Instead of cementing the unity of the Peninsula, they merely reinforced the political division between tribes, enabling the Romans to establish their hold over Spain.

Tartessos and Turdetania

Tartessos constitutes a special case in Iberian history, which tends to contradict our assertions. In the seventh and sixth centuries B.C., Tartessos was apparently an empire based on the

Iberian civilisation: political and social structures

Guadalquivir valley, which gave it its geographical unity. It spread beyond the Sierra Morena to the north, and Avienus tells us that it extended as far as Cape de la Nao, taking in the 'Mastian' region. The richness of the soil and subsoil gave it a solid economic basis. There was no ethnic unity, since Indo-European elements (the Celts) lived alongside the autochthonous Tartessian-Turdulan-Turdetanians and the immigrant Semites. And, to judge by the systems of writing used in Lower and Upper Andalusia, two languages prevailed.

Tradition, as reflected by Herodotus, has it that this 'Tartessian empire' was at first governed by a king, Arganthonios, who reigned for 120 years, from 670 to about 550. This king's supposed longevity, which became proverbial, was certainly exaggerated. The long span must have embraced several successive reigns or simply expressed the strong continuity of the monarchy whose seat was the city of Tartessos. The worthy centenarian sovereign must have been fond of the Greeks, since he received Kolaios the Samian with warmth, approved of the foundation of Mainaké in his domain and donated money to rebuild the walls of Phocea. His pro-Greek attitude sought perhaps to counterbalance the influence of troublesome neighbours, the Phoenicians at Gadir and the Carthaginians.

This Tartessian monarchy probably did not survive the Carthaginian victory at Alalia (540). In any case there is no written mention of Tartessos after that date. Later, Turdetania was divided into independent kingdoms in ceaseless conflict with one another, whose military power was measured by the number of strongholds owned. These rival kingdoms signed treaties of alliance first with Barca and later with the Romans, on condition of being subsidised by them.

We cannot be sure that these small Andalusian kings possessed absolute power even over a limited territory. In the top stratum of the social hierarchy were latifundiaries; that is to say, great landowners and mine-owners. Closely con-

nected with this powerful aristocracy were the rich Semitic
merchants, and from early on there arose a wealthy class of
Semitised natives, from among whom Hannibal chose his
wife. Under such conditions these petty kings were probably
merely the agents of the powerful landowners.

The economic exploitation of the country presupposed a
large number of slaves working in mines and on great estates,
but we have proof of the existence of a class of free wage-
earning peasants and miners and even of small landowners.
The social hierarchy may have embraced castes ranging from
slaves to great landowners, but obviously the system did not
ensure social stability. Fugitive slaves and peasants, dis-
possessed by greedy nobles, most probably joined the armed
bands which ravaged the border regions of Turdetania and
inland Spain.

The south-east and the Spanish Levant

It is customary to contrast the political and social regime of
Turdetania, a monarchy, with that of the south-east and the
Levant, which was apparently democratic. This idea is
based on the case of Saguntum where the Senate negotiated
with the Romans and sought their aid when Hannibal laid
siege to their citadel. The government of Saguntum resembled
that of a Greek *polis*. One is tempted to apply the same pattern
to the host of small city states, consisting of one or several
oppida which covered the region between the Segura and the
plain of Saguntum and perhaps further north.

We know little of their history apart from the incessant
wars that ravaged them. While their political structure was
unquestionably influenced by Greece, it would be going too
far to make any comparison with the Greek state. Assemblies
tended to disintegrate as a result of the general instability. At
a later date some cities had kings who were a pale reflection
of Hellenistic sovereigns, such as Edegon, king of the Edetani,
who was probably elected at Edeta (Liria?). All things
considered, the ruling oligarchies of the south-east probably

performed a political role similar to that of the Turdetanian aristocracy, except that we have no evidence of any Senate in Turdetania.

The social structure of the south-east and the Spanish Levant seems to have differed from that of Turdetania. Economic power in these regions was not based on large estates, which must only have existed in the highlands of the *Campus Spartarius*. The lowlands and the *huertas* were presumably parcelled out with less disparity between rich and poor. Nevertheless the luxurious jewellery that has been discovered by archaeologists bears witness to the existence of higher social strata.

We know even less about the political and social structure of the regions of the interior and the north-east, Aragon and Catalonia, in which Celts mingled with Iberian tribes. It is only known that the latter sometimes formed provisional confederations under military leaders, or *caudillos*.

These confederations, inspired by patriotism, were rash enough to attack the armies of Hamilcar Barca. He once defeated them but was soon afterwards forced to retreat hurriedly before the united Oretani. It was then, it will be recalled, that he met his death by drowning in the Júcar.

The unstable elements in the population of the interior – the rootless wanderers from Turdetania – also served as mercenaries in the Carthaginian armies from the third century onwards and subsequently in those of Rome. Livy tells us how recruiting agents enlisted the unemployed by bribing them with an initial bonus.

Iberians always liked fighting for its own sake, but they were impelled to enlist by the lure of plunder and by the promise of land to army veterans. They were valued for their courage and loyalty, and Carthage took advantage of the rivalry between Spanish tribes by recruiting some to fight others. But the mercenaries were engaged chiefly in battlefields outside Spain by Carthage, which was always short of men, and by Greek cities. In Syracuse particularly, the tyrant Dionysius employed them in both his army and personal bodyguard (480 B.C.).

Hannibal's troops were largely made up of Iberians and Celts. A. García y Bellido has put forward the hypothesis that mercenaries even fought in Greece itself and that they contributed in no small measure to the spread of Greek influence in Spain. This is quite probable, and one would like to know what proportion of the Greek objects found in Iberia had been brought back as souvenirs by soldiers.

Dress, adornment and social types

The small bronze statuettes which are our richest source of information about social types in Spain came mainly from the sanctuaries of the Sierra Morena, the region which forms a junction between the Tartessian domain (Upper Andalusia), the Celtic lands (Meseta) and the south-east (the Segura mountains). Thus the picture derived from these bronzes is that of the composite society that frequented these sanctuaries, coming from every corner of ancient Spain. It is thus impossible to relate this picture to any particular region. However it enables us to pick out certain social types which existed in one or several regions of Iberia.

Bronze figurines of the Oretanian sanctuaries and other monuments of Iberian art suggest a division of society into broad categories which apply to both sexes. As regards men, these categories do not correspond to social classes nor even to divisions between soldiers and civilians, since warriors came from every category except that of the priesthood. It thus seems artificial – and the texts confirm this view – to distinguish a warrior class, for the term had no meaning in Iberian society. Take horsemen, for instance. The figure of a rider from Salobral, now in the Louvre, wore a helmet with a great crest, like the one from La Bastida (pl. I). This is not to be identified with the three-plumed helmet described by Strabo. Both carry a *falcata* (falchion) and a *caetra* (buckler), but one wears a cloak and the other does not. Others again are bare-headed, in short tunics, armed with a *falcata* (fig. 4) or two lances (fig. 5). Finally there are horsemen carrying no weapons, bare-headed or wearing a diadem, sometimes dressed in richly decorated tunics (fig. 6). The hair-style of these latter resembles that of the 'non-tonsured priests'. They were probably great personages. This variety of horsemen, these permutations of dress and of arms, lead us to conclude that there was probably no class of knights or horsemen among the Iberians as was the case in Athens or Rome. Horses must have been plentiful and cheap enough for everyone to be able to ride. In fact, according to Strabo, there were no mounted corps in the Iberian army, where

4 Warrior on horseback. Third century. Height 9·3 cm. Valencia de Don Juan Museum, Madrid)

infantry and cavalry mingled in battle. He adds that the horsemen were extremely skilful. They could make their horses kneel, probably to conceal them from the enemy. Sometimes they would ride two on the same mount, and the 'passenger' sitting pillion would leap to the ground to attack or defend himself on meeting an adversary.

A second category, almost as diversified as that of the horsemen, comprises men on foot wearing cloaks. These include members of the highest ranks of society. We find for instance a figure wearing a wig (fig. 7) with a double cloak, made out of a rectangle of cloth folded in two and fastened on the right shoulder. Another wears a sumptuous garment

5 Despeñaperros (Santa Elena, Jaén). Bronze warrior on horseback. Sixth or fifth century. Height 6 cm. (National Archaeological Museum, Madrid)

6 Opposite: *Despeñaperros (Santa Elena, Jaén). Bronze horseman. Fourth century. Height 5·2 cm.* (National Archaeological Museum, Madrid)
7 Below, left: *Despeñaperros (Santa Elena, Jaén). Bronze statuette of votary. Sixth century. Height 11·2 cm.* (National Archaeological Museum, Madrid)
8 Below, right: *Province of Murcia (?). Bronze statuette of warrior in draped mantle. Roman period. Height 9·5 cm.* (National Archaeological Museum, Madrid)

with a broad, heavy fringed border (fig. 8). Another warrior is dressed less grandly, yet he also wears a double cloak (fig. 9). Others wear only single, shorter cloaks, fastened by fibulae, sometimes with a small flap hanging behind in points. The size and style of cloak are obviously a sign of wealth, and the colours of these garments must have been brilliant and varied, to judge by the fragment of a stone bust found at Elche, which shows a bright red cloak fastened on the right shoulder with a big annular fibula which must have been an elaborate bronze ornament. However, the cloak worn by the

men of the interior was commonly black, the usual colour of sheep's wool in those regions. This garment served a variety of purposes: as a protection from cold and heat, as a rug at night, or, folded in two or in four, as a saddle for bareback riders. Its origin is unknown. Strabo calls it a *sagum*, like the Celtic garment. But the Iberian mantle was generally bigger than the *sagum* and worn differently; it was fastened on the right shoulder and passed under the left arm, leaving the left shoulder uncovered.

Under the mantle, men, apart from priests, wore a short tunic, the style of which betokened the wearer's wealth. It was probably the poor man's sole garment and consisted of a piece of woollen or linen cloth with a round hole or a slit through which the head was passed. It was fastened at the waist with a buckled belt. The tunics of the affluent were equipped with made-up sleeves and were long enough for the two ends to be sewn together between the legs. See for instance the tunic of the embossed figure in the Museo Valencia de Don Juan (fig. 10) and that of the rider with the diadem (fig. 6). Livy speaks of the dazzling picture made by Hannibal's Iberian troops at the battle of Cannae, in their white linen tunics edged with purple. These were in fact rather stiff, heavy garments which acted somewhat as cuirasses, or at any rate stood up well to cuts.

The short tunic which seems to have been the national dress of Iberians in every province from Turdetania to Catalonia was probably of Oriental origin. The Phoenicians had worn it from remote times and it was adopted by the Carthaginians. The Iberians probably started wearing it at the beginning of the first millennium, if one accepts the evidence of the earliest sculptures.

The social category that can clearly be distinguished is that of the priesthood. These are always depicted in an attitude of prayer, standing rigidly, their heads tonsured or bound with a fillet. They are richly dressed in flounced linen robes and a mantle, also flounced, draped over the left shoulder,

9 Despeñaperros (?). Bronze statuette of warrior. Fourth century. Height 6·7 cm.
(Valencia de Don Juan Museum, Madrid)

with a small flap adorned with a tassel and sometimes a veil, all trimmed with copious braids (fig. 11). Priestesses were similarly dressed, apart from the tonsure or hair-style (fig. 12). Both priests and priestesses wore characteristic jewellery, serpent-shaped bracelets and necklaces bearing amulets like that from Aliseda (fig. 13). The statuettes representing such figures are found only at Despeñaperros and Castellar. They are undoubtedly of Oriental origin: the flounced robes, the shape of the body with neck and head bent forward are also found both in the East and at Carthage. Scholars have wondered whether they actually portrayed

10 Meseta (?). Thin sheet of gold, repoussé work. (Valencia de Don Juan Museum, Madrid)

11 Despeñaperros (Santa Elena, Jaén). Bronze statuette of priest. Sixth or fifth century. Height 8·6 cm. (National Archaeological Museum, Madrid)

priests of Oretanian sanctuaries or rather Eastern priests
from some sanctuary of Baal-Tanit or Melkart in the south
of the Peninsula.

A woman's attire was more indicative of social rank.
Figures of 'ladies', of which the Dama de Elche is the most
remarkable representative (pl. V), have been found in
great abundance at El Cerro de los Santos and at Despeñaperros. They can be recognised by their fantastically
complex garments and sumptuous jewellery. The outer
garment consists of a great veil hanging over the high head-
dress or down the back, a shawl and a mantle draped over the

*12 Despeñaperros (Santa Elena, Jaén). Bronze statuette of 'priestess'. Sixth or
fifth century. Height 10·1 cm.* (National Archaeological Museum, Madrid)

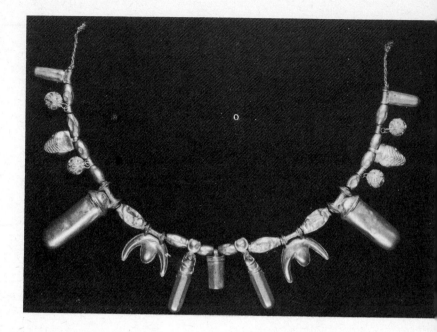

left shoulder (the only difference with that of the men), with or without a flap. Underneath these is worn a dress with a straight neckline, sometimes with a small collar fastened by a fibula, or else a slanting neckline. Finally, hanging down in front and behind, covering the heels, one or several petticoats or a train complete the outfit (fig. 14).

A woman of rank wore a great deal of jewellery: huge discs over her ears, in which presumably she concealed her hair, a diadem on her forehead, several rows of necklaces with many pendants containing amulets (larger than those of the priests), and rings on her fingers. This was certainly the costume worn by queens and noble ladies. The less elaborately dressed ladies portrayed in the smaller bronzes often wear a pointed head-dress reminiscent of the medieval *hennin*. This may have concealed the rod round which, according to Strabo, their hair was wound, the whole being enveloped in a black veil.

The humbler type of woman wore a sort of flat tabor-shaped head-dress, suggestive of the cylindrical *polos* of

14 *Cerro de los Santos*
(Montealegre, Albacete).
The 'Gran Dama' carved
in limestone. Fourth century.
Height 1·36 metres.
(National Archaeological
Museum, Madrid)

Iberian civilisation: political and social structures

Rhodian and Oriental women, or a low crescent-shaped mitre. Sometimes hair hung in long plaits over the shoulders. Others had wigs with thick braids ending in ornaments (fig. 15). All wore a single dress with or without a train, and few jewels. Short skirts already existed, at any rate in the south-east (fig. 16), and were worn with boots with turned-down tops that have quite a modern look.

It is clear from these more or less realistic figures that Iberian society included a very rich class, whose dress and ornaments were magnificent, whose members were to be found in all the categories we have considered and to which the priestly caste belonged specifically. The rest of the population was less sharply divided, and it would be a mistake to insist on discerning clearly defined social categories for the reasons already mentioned. Obviously the very poor are never depicted since these figurines were individual ex-votos; indeed the needy would have lacked the means to offer more than purely schematic figures. In any case they would presumably have presented a somewhat embellished image of themselves.

Behaviour and temperament

It is particularly difficult to outline the Iberians' character. In this respect archaeological documents are not always helpful. Iberian inscriptions on *stelae*, vases and leaden tablets (fig. 2) are still awaiting their translator. In any case it is doubtful if they could teach us much. Thus the writings of antiquity are the most important source of our knowledge of the psychology of the ancient Spaniards.

The description of 'barbarians', whether Iberians, Carthaginians, Gauls, Germans, Scythians or Persians, by Greek or Roman writers is tinged to some degree with prejudice. In Graeco-Roman antiquity there was a stock image of the 'barbarian'. Not only did he speak an unintelligible language, as his name indicates – 'barbarus' is etymologically onomatopoeic – but he had exaggerated faults and qualities. Under

16 La Luz (Verdolay, Murcia). Bronze statuette of votaress. Third or second century. Height 14·5 cm. (Archaeological Museum, Barcelona)

15 Despeñaperros (Santa Elena, Jaén). Detail from a bronze statuette of a votary. Sixth century. Height 11·2 cm. (National Archaeological Museum, Madrid)

such conditions it is hard to isolate the authentic elements in a conventional description, the more so when the author admits that 'the same *mores* are to be found among the Iberians, Celts, Thracians and Scythians'!

There is little chance of being able to reconstruct the physical appearance of the Iberians, which varied considerably from region to region. Strabo's gentle, Romanised Turdetanians must have been quite different from the rough highlanders of the interior, who were tall and slender, terrible to look at (according to Livy), with an abundance of wavy hair. The bronze figures portray men with long heads and rather short legs, some slender women and others generously proportioned and copiously bedecked. Their evidence must be taken with caution, for they are patently unrealistic.

It appears from the texts, and to some extent from pictorial and sculptural material, that war was the Iberians' main activity, except for those of the south; inter-tribal warfare was endemic, a fierce, total war, in which villages and crops were destroyed by fire. Collective massacres, the sacrifice of prisoners and the suicide of the vanquished were common. But the battle itself must have been an extraordinary sight: savages, sometimes naked, brandishing weapons and uttering shrill cries as they danced to frighten the foe. One can imagine their terrifying effect on the Roman troops, whom they often defeated before Spain was completely subdued. When war was not raging they organised fights and tournaments between horsemen and foot-warriors to the accompaniment of flutes and horns, as we see in a vase-painting from Liria (fig. 17). Sometimes they even staged set battles.

Side by side with incessant wars, brigandage was common, practised by whole hordes of vagrants who plundered harvests and lifted cattle under the leadership of a chieftain to whom all were bound by *devotio*. These bands were probably hard to distinguish from actual troops, for they generally attacked neighbouring peoples and carried home their booty.

They were probably always more abundant in the interior than in Turdetania or the Levant.

This love of war and violence was naturally allied with exceptional courage. One can therefore understand why the Romans' task in subduing men of this calibre was so formidable. When under siege their resistance was unshakeable, and the most horrible stories are current in ancient writings about their behaviour on such occasions. Sooner than capitulate or leave spoils for the enemy, the Iberians destroyed all and then committed mass suicide.

The stubborn resistance of the Celtiberians at Numancia is well known; the courage of the men of Astapa (Estepa, Seville) is even more remarkable, being bound up with that typical trait of the Iberian character – their unswerving fidelity to a sworn oath. Livy tells in detail how the city, having formed an alliance with the Cathaginians, remained faithful to them when all Turdetania had deserted them. Once besieged, the men of Astapa collected all their possessions in a pile on which they put the women and children and to which they then set fire. Having attempted one last desperate sortie, they then returned to fling themselves into the furnace.

Strabo gives other examples of these holocausts, which were far from uncommon. And while the men showed unparalleled endurance in warfare – the Iberian mercenaries being as keen in battle as they were tireless on marches or in vigil – that of the women was equally remarkable; they helped their husbands and looked after their homes; while working in the fields they sometimes gave birth unattended, by the side of a stream in which they would bathe their infant, and immediately go back to work again.

We have little information about their diet. The mountain people drank beer and water and fed traditionally on goats' flesh, butter and acorn bread. But they must have added the products of the chase (deer, roebuck, wild boar, rabbits) and of their animal husbandry. The men of the plains had more varied food, as the list given by Athenaeus, following Polybius, indicates: barley, wheat, wine, veal, mutton, pork, kid, hare, various fish, asparagus and figs.

Strabo describes a banquet at which the procedure surprised him greatly. For one thing, instead of lying on couches as the Greeks did, the guests ate sitting down on seats prepared in the walls all round the room. After eating, everyone started drinking (here the parallel with the Greek banquet is evident) and, to the sound of flute and horn, the men began to dance, alternately jumping and crouching or moving round rhythmically in a ring. Among the Bastetani, women joined in with the men. The Liria vases have handed down to us a faithful picture of such scenes, which reveal the other side of the fierce Iberian character. We can imagine the noisy merry-making, when the wine flowed freely during the warm Spanish nights. During the Roman period the dancing girls of Cadiz were famous for their lascivious suppleness and for the songs which they accompanied with castanets.

The role of music and the dance was evidently considerable. Dancing warriors were certainly accompanied by musicians, as were those who took part in tournaments (pl. II); they would move into battle rhythmically, beating their round bucklers. Excavation in Numancia has disclosed the clay horns represented in the Liria vase-paintings. They are primitive instruments, closer to the serpent than to the horn. The flutes on the other hand conform to the Graeco-Roman model of the *aulos*. We do not know whether this instrument accompanied the recital of epic poems and of those paeans sung in battle which formed the basis of Tartessian literature – of which nothing is left but Strabo's recollection.

Religion

Most of the musical scenes depicted are evidently magical or expiatory in character, including that of the tournament from Liria (fig. 17). Archaeology has thus provided us with a

17 Cerro de San Miguel (Liria, Valencia).
Detail from a handleless krater. *Second*
century. Overall height 30 cm. External
diameter 43 cm.

precious sum of evidence, undoubtedly richer than the sparse
contribution of ancient writers. Nevertheless Iberian religion,
in spite of recent studies, remains largely obscure. We have
seen how important the major sanctuaries had been in the
formation and evolution of Iberian art. They must also be
envisaged as the country's essential religious centres, at any
rate between Upper Andalusia and the Spanish Levant.

It is very hard to explain the gap in Lower Andalusia and
the north-east, where the sanctuaries (if we are to trust the
monuments of Azaila) may have been situated actually within
the towns, although the present state of archaeological
prospecting precludes any certainty on this point. The

attribution of any particular type of sanctuary to a specific region thus seems highly problematical. We know that there were cave sanctuaries in Upper Andalusia, or more accurately speaking in the Oretanian region, on the Andalusian slope of the Sierra Morena. The three basic requirements for a consecrated place were: the cave, the spring and the hilltop or sacred wood, according to different authors. It was only later, from the fifth century onwards, that the construction of temples was envisaged.

The town was built last, at any rate in the case of Despeña-perros. In fact this pattern of development is quite classic and was repeated many times in Greece and elsewhere. The only thing lacking in Iberia was the notion of the god's territory, the *temenos*; possibly the surrounding wall of Despeñaperros may mark the limits of that domain. Clearly the sanctuary ceased before very long to be associated with rocks and caves and came to conform to the general type of the great Mediterranean sanctuaries.

In contrast with the cave-sanctuaries of Andalusia, the religious constructions of the south-east have sometimes been considered as having no connection with any cave. But things were not quite so straightforward. At La Luz the sanctuary had been built on a high place between two ravines and the spring was nearby. At El Cigarralejo and at Cerro de los Santos – where the temple may have been merely a treasure-house for storing the offerings of the faithful – there was probably some primitive cult of the mountain tops, later replaced by that of an ill-defined deity. Moreover the construction of the temple or religious building was here, as in Andalusia, later than the establishment of the cult. It is not impossible that a sacred cave may some day be discovered in the Spanish Levant; witness the strange little votive grotto of terracotta found in the neighbourhood of Alicante.

The nature of the gods that haunted these sanctuaries has often been debated, and it has never proved possible to give them a name. Yet we find traces of a highly developed pantheon among the Iberians who soon accepted Oriental and Semitic deities, and later assimilated them to the gods of Greece and Rome.

This was the case for instance with the cult of Melkart-Herakles-Hercules at Cadiz, which spread widely throughout Lower Andalusia and along the coast as far as Cartagena right into Roman times. This deity gave advice and foretold the future by means of the dreams he inspired in those who consulted him, among whom were Hannibal and Caesar. The cult of the Cathaginian goddess Tanit-Caelestis was equally widespread. She was assimilated to Hera-Demeter-Juno, with a variety of functions, including the safeguarding of human fertility and that of the land. Baal-Kronos-Saturn probably received less honour, though in certain Iberian cemeteries there have been found traces of human sacrifice which may be connected with his bloodthirsty cult.

Many other names might be added to these: Astarte-Aphrodite, Allath-Athena, Chousor-Hephaistos, Salambo and so on. Despite their familiar names these deities are somewhat ill-defined. This is shown by the way they have been assimilated to a number of Greek gods or goddesses at once, which makes it difficult to recognise them. The same thing happened with the Celtic pantheon, which was probably introduced into Iberia with the great Celtic immigrations of the first millennium B.C., and also through the contact between Iberians and Celts in the interior of the country.

This imprecision seems to be a fundamental characteristic of primitive Iberian religion. The gods had very diverse, not to say universal, functions. Their outlines remain vague. This is true incidentally of many primitive religions.

However, we possess images of the Iberian gods which, even if we cannot give them names, enlighten us as to their broad functions.

A first category includes the fertility goddesses and the 'mothers'. The statuette from Galera (fig. 18) is an expressive example of this cult. Others represent a mother suckling or

18 Galera *(Granada). Alabaster statuette of goddess. Seventh century. Height 18 cm.* (National Archaeological Museum, Madrid)

19 La Serreta *(Alcoy, Alicante).* Pinax *of terracotta. Third or second century. Length 18·5 cm.* (Archaeological Museum, Alcoy)

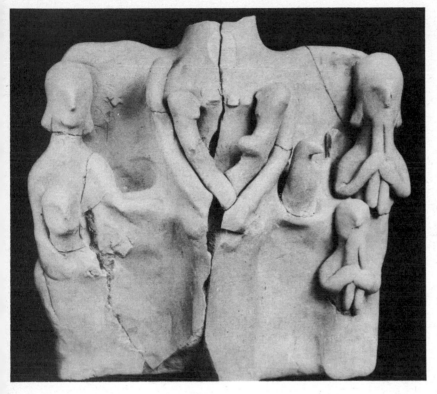

carrying children, like the terracotta figure from La Albufereta, closely akin to Graeco-Punic models. Even more significant is the seated mother from La Serreta (fig. 19), suckling two children; she is accompanied by her divine attribute, a bird. The two groups on either side reinforce the meaning of the central group. On the left, a mother and her child – possibly the dedicators of the votive object – and on the right the same figures, accompanying the sacrifice on their twin pipes.

A second series of deities is represented by the winged goddesses surrounded by attributes associated with the cults of the underworld, such as snakes (figs. 20 and 21). They also appear in the role of 'mistress of animals' between two horses. As we shall see, there was also a 'master of horses' with one (fig. 22) or two faces (fig. 23) in Iberia, and a sanctuary

20 *La Alcudia* (*Elche, Alicante*). Oenochoe
(*detail*). *Third or second century. Total
height of vase 47 cm.* (Municipal Museum,
Elche)

21 *La Alcudia* (*Elche, Alicante*). *Detail of
fig. 20*

for horses at El Cigarralejo (Mula, Murcia). The same deity, probably, is depicted on one of the medallions from Los Almadenes de Pozoblanco (fig. 24). They all share a vaguely protective character, based on some telluric cult, akin to the fertility cults to which we have already referred.

More instructive is the *patera* from Tivisa, which depicts a series of mythological scenes with themes of a protective character (fig. 25). A first group shows a man seated in majesty, offering an object to a child. This may be the beginning of the myth; the figure is clearly that of a god. Beside him a crouching boy is surrounded by three boars.

22 Mogón (Jaén). 'Master of the animals' in stone relief. Fourth or third century. Length 72 cm. (Archaeological Museum, Jaén)

Next come the theme of the rider and that of the wild beast attacking a bull. Further on a winged daemon is holding a candelabra, on which an eagle is perched. Another daemon is about to sacrifice a sheep, while an acolyte carries a *ryton* [a vessel to collect the blood] and a leafy branch. A final scene represents a centaur with a wild cat and a boar.

Most of these themes are clearly of Mediterranean origin: the seated god, the fighting animals, the centaur, the winged daemons, all show a remote Oriental inspiration. But their meaning, or more exactly the use made of it here, the Iberian interpretation of it, escapes us. Some of the themes

23 Villaricos (Almeria). 'Master of the animals' in stone relief. Third century. Length 36 cm. (Archaeological Museum, Barcelona).

are protective symbols, others have an obvious funerary significance: the boar, a common Celtic funerary symbol, the rider, the centaur – beings who lead souls towards their last dwelling. Their presence indicates that this *patera* was used for funerary libations.

The symbols protective of the dead, such as those on the Tivisa *patera*, represent only a small fraction of the symbolic signs to be found in Iberian pictorial art. These shed light on a basic characteristic of the religious beliefs and superstitions of the Iberians. Some depict human figures, sometimes in association with animals. Among those that have been discovered are fighting warriors, the master or mistress of animals, the rider, the nude warrior, the naked man with an exaggeratedly large penis, the sexual organ alone (phallic amulets), the eye, the hand (the last two discovered in hundreds in sanctuaries) and the 'sign of Tanit' – a T-shaped cross surmounted by a circle.

A second animal series includes battles between animals and also individual creatures such as horses, deer, wild boars, lions, bulls, wolves, birds and beasts of prey, snakes, fish and aquatic insects, as well as fantastic animals such as griffins, sphinxes, centaurs and dragons. Some of these are used as symbols of the elements: the bird = air, the fish, the water-boatman = water, the snake = earth. Plants play a part too: palm trees, branches, the 'tree of life', the lotus flower, and their stylised derivatives, palm leaves, palmettes and rosettes.

Finally there are astral symbols: the sun, the moon, the crescent. All the possibilities offered by Mediterranean symbolism have been used. But the Iberians added to these other, more abstract symbols: twisted or plaited elements (for instance, braids, 'breast cords', belts, collars, knots) which appear to have had a magic significance; and the amulets worn particularly by priests (fig. 11), since they were obviously more threatened by evil spirits than other men. A symbolic meaning has even been attributed to the buckle that fastened a warrior's belt. Presented as an ex-voto offering with his

24 Los Almadenes de Pozoblanco (Cordoba).
Silver medallions. Third century. Diameters
from 2·2 cm. to 2·8 cm. (Archaeological
Museum, Cordoba)

weapons, it appears on the figurines, inordinately magnified.
It was in fact itself decorated with protective symbols.

A whole section of these symbolic elements belongs more
especially to the cult of the dead; examples of these are seen
on the Tivisa *patera*. We find them again on the Liria vases:
the theme of the deer-hunt, akin to that of the wild boar
hunt, snakes and fishes and a whole series of elements

connected with water. The ivy leaf and the lotus leaf suggest 'life' in the world beyond, a sort of renewal, or rebirth, which is also symbolised in tombs by the presence of an egg (an ostrich egg, if one was rich) sometimes accompanied by the warrior's sword or lance, folded in three. In his after-life the dead man evidently required sustenance, which was supplied by libations of wine or water mixed with honey; containers for these were sometimes shown borne on the back of a humble donkey.

The votive offerings laid in sanctuaries undoubtedly reveal through their symbolism something of the Iberian religion. But we learn even more about it through what has been called (by R. Lantier) the 'grammar of gestures' in figurines and statuettes. These gestures also help us to form a clearer notion of the deities worshipped in these sanctuaries. Worshippers are shown standing to attention with hands held out, palm upward, as though to receive the beneficent favours dispensed by the god, or else with a single hand raised in salutation. Sometimes they even seem to bend the knee in token of respect, in a movement akin to the crouching attitude of the dancer noted by Strabo or the 'wild boar keeper' of the Tivisa *patera*. Others hold or display their sexual organs. Women press their breasts. The worshippers offer their god, with one or both hands, a fruit, a cake, or a small victim such as a bird, a dog or a rabbit. Sometimes they pray with one hand and offer with the other, as though giving in order to receive. All, or almost all, are barefooted. These gestures are to a great extent borrowed from the primitive ritual of the Mediterranean, already established by the Bronze Age. Their meaning is known: they are generally addressed to deities of the underworld, who have control over the fertility of men, animals and plants. The Iberians attributed to them protective powers over the world of the living and the dead, and furthermore healing powers which they exercised over the sick pilgrims who visited their holy

25 Tivisa (Tarragona). Silver patera *with gold plating. External diameter 17·2 cm.* (Archaeological Museum, Barcelona)

place. That is all we know about them. Did the Iberians themselves know more about these gods, whose power over them was limitless? Did they ever give them a face or a name? Remember the prayer of the earliest Romans, contemporary with the Iberians, as related by Ovid: 'O thou, whether thou beest god or goddess, grant me thy blessing!'

CHAPTER 5
Towns and architecture

A large number of habitation centres have been recognised and excavated throughout Iberian Spain, from the Rhône to the Guadiana, from the coast to the inland regions. Outside these settlements, isolated buildings and sites yielding Iberian objects are relatively rare. Undoubtedly Iberian culture was the product of group-living. The contrary would be surprising; with a few exceptions, such settlements were the rule all along the Mediterranean coast. In the case of Spain this mode of living was dictated by various causes: the climate which necessitated concentration around sources of water, the insecurity which made isolation dangerous and the authoritarian political regime which, whether monarchical or not, was better served by having its people grouped around the local ruler.

The need to exploit the land, whether for agriculture or for pasturing, generally obliged men to live in groups. Judging by scattered finds, isolated dwellings must have existed only in the fertile plains along the coast from the Spanish Levant to Catalonia. But presumably these were close to some centre which would serve as refuge against any threat coming by land or sea. The Iberian settlement was thus determined by geographical conditions as much as by history. It must be seen as a permanent condition, for even today in rural areas of Spain, villages are sometimes separated by miles of apparently deserted country.

A first problem arises when we seek to assess the size of these settlements in pre-Roman Iberia. Are they to be described as towns or villages? In view of the multiplicity

of these centres, can one speak of an urban civilisation, as is usually done when dealing with the period of the Roman occupation? To answer this question one must abandon present-day criteria which distinguish between towns and villages according to the number and the occupations of their inhabitants. We know in fact that certain towns in the ancient world would today be no more than large villages. Furthermore, information is lacking about the size of population of these Iberian settlements. Archaeologists and historians must ultimately judge by the surface occupied by dwellings within, and possibly outside, the walls of a settlement.

When architectural remains are not easily discernible, the settlement's perimeter must be assessed by means of other

27 Below: *Aerial view of Tarragona. Note the outline of the 'cyclopean' and Roman wall around the old town. The sea is at the bottom of the photograph*

traces of human habitation, especially pottery. It has been possible in this way to ascertain that the most extensive and important towns were about 10 hectares in area: Indika, the native settlement which was a twin to the Nea Polis of Ampurias (Gerona) (fig. 26) was possibly smaller than Iberian Tarragona (fig. 27) and Burriach (Cabrera de Mataró, Barcelona), which covered an area of 10 to 12 hectares at the time of the Roman conquest. Sant Juliá de Ramis (Gerona) followed them closely with its 7 hectares.

Far behind came a whole series of moderate-sized settlements such as La Bastida (Mogente, Valencia), 5 hectares, Ullastret (Gerona) and Tivisa (Tarragona), the acropolis of Despeñaperros (Santa Elena, Jaén), 4 hectares, La Serreta

(Alcoy, Alicante), 2·5 hectares, etc. Most towns in fact covered an area of one hectare or less: Iberian Azaila (Teruel) (plan, p. 83) and San Antonio de Calaceite (Teruel) about one hectare, Puig Castellar (Santa Coloma de Gramanet, Barcelona) 6,000 square metres, Olius (Lérida) 8,000 square metres, El Taratrato (Alcañiz, Teruel) (plan p. 85), 1,000 square metres. Yet the fortress of Rhocina (Sot de Ferrer, Castellón de la Plana) was no larger than 800 square metres. It would thus be rash to judge the importance of a settlement merely by its surface area.

In architecture, as in other arts, Iberian civilisation was subject to Mediterranean influence without on that account abandoning pre-existing indigenous or primitive techniques

It is the respective importance of external contributions and indigenous traditions, varying according to regions and sites that characterises the different types of Iberian settlement.

Urban sites

The most widespread type of habitation centre was a fortified *oppidum* on a hill. But there was no uniformity about these; of varying size, they were adapted to the character of their situation, and also no doubt to regional needs, as can be imagined in so vast a territory.

As the map shows, the number of *oppida* in the interior of the country was large. To mention only the most famous Osuna (Seville), Castellones de Ceal (Jaén), La Bastida (Mogente, Valencia), San Miguel de Liria (Valencia) El Taratrato (Alcañiz, Teruel), San Antonio de Calaceite (Teruel), Azaila (Teruel), Tivisa (Tarragona), Olérdola (Tarragona), Burriach (Cabrera de Mataró, Barcelona) and Puig Castellar on the outskirts of Barcelona. But apart from these *oppida* we find hill towns, fortified or not, associated with sanctuaries, as at Despeñaperros (Santa Elena, Jaén (plan, p. 84), Cabecico del Tesoro (Verdolay, Murcia) or E Cigarralejo (Mula, Murcia).

Besides these towns there were a few habitation centres in

Plan of the Roman township of Azaila showing traces of the original settlement, perhaps dating from pre-Iberian times

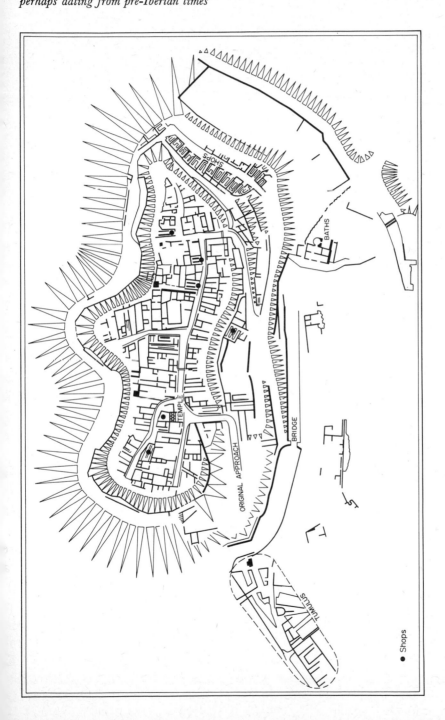

SHOPS

BATHS

TEMPLE

ORIGINAL APPROACH

BRIDGE

TUMULUS

● Shops

Towns and architecture

Below: *Acropolis of Despeñaperros (Jaén), a typical Iberian settlement*

Opposite: *The Iberian village of El Taratrato, excavated half a century ago. Material recovered from the site is of poor quality, though there are traces of economic life in the form of shops, one of them a bakery*

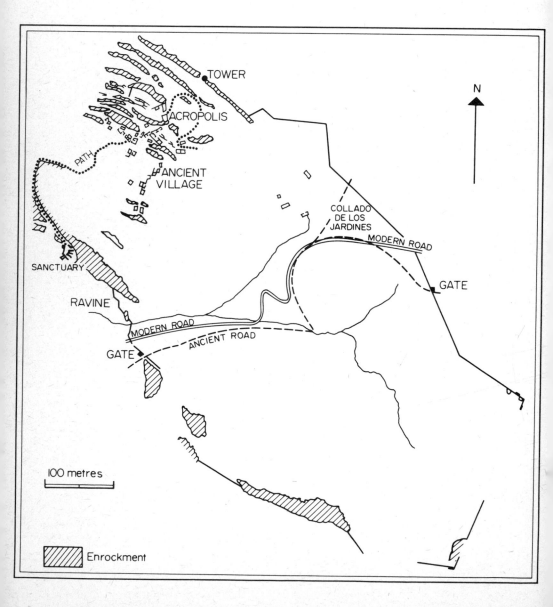

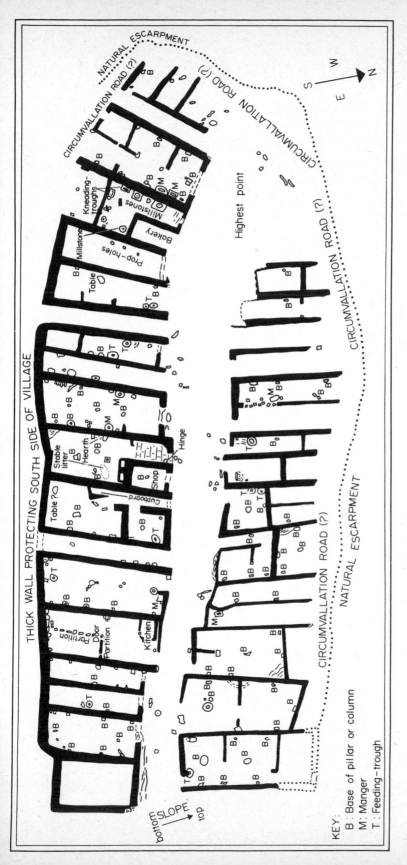

85

KEY:
B: Base of pillar or column
M: Manger
T: Feeding-trough

the plains, such as that at La Alcudia-Elche (Alicante), where the famous 'Dama' was discovered. This was inhabited from the Bronze Age until Roman times. Excavations currently proceeding may well reveal sizeable ramparts. We may also cite El Carambolo, a settlement close to Seville, where several superimposed strata have been discovered. Ullastret in Catalonia, the intermediary between the *oppidum* and the plain settlement, is a fortress clinging to the side of a small hill some 30 metres high.

Seaports form a special category; they probably arose as a result of the indigenous coastal trade, but they developed chiefly through contact with Phocean and Greek colonisers and traders. Such was the famous Indika or Tarragona, established on a hill near the shore, surrounded by its 'cyclopean' walls (fig. 27). There were also large *oppida* close to the sea, such as Castell de la Fosca (Palamós, Gerona) or the Iberian settlement on the hill of Montjuich, now inside the city of Barcelona.

All these towns or villages were situated near a thoroughfare or overlooking a valley or a mountain pass. Sometimes indeed the *oppidum* was particularly difficult of access, being built at the junction of several ridges. This was the case with Puig Castellar whose territory extended over several valleys. Other sites were more favourably situated; thus the famous Saguntum (Valencia), the capture of which by Hannibal was one of the causes of the great war between Carthage and Rome, had every advantage: an acropolis with steep flanks making defence easy, standing in the middle of a rich irrigable plain, on the main coastal road a few kilometres from the sea, on which the ships of traders and colonisers from Greece and Carthage sailed.

Nevertheless certain *oppida* had a space problem. Situated as they were on a height, they found it difficult to expand when the population increased without jeopardising the effectiveness of their defence system. Such was the prevailing insecurity that it was out of the question to let the town spread into the valley or the plain. It was found necessary to make the best possible use of the high ground by cutting new dwellings out of the rock, or building them on artificial embankments and enclosing them within an extension of the existing wall. San Antonio de Calaceite was enlarged in this way. Another solution was simply to built a protective wall behind which to shelter in times of danger.

The geographical distribution of Iberian settlements shows a certain disproportion between the south-east, Catalonia and the Levant, where they are numerous, and Andalusia where they are much fewer. This is due to the fact that archaeological prospection is far less advanced in Andalusia than elsewhere in Spain.

Historic reality is quite different. In fact there are so many indications that the Tartessian region was densely populated that one can unhesitatingly locate the wealthiest cities there, those of which ancient writers, Strabo in particular, give such glowing descriptions: Ilipa (Alcalá del Río), Astigis (Ecija), Carmo (Carmona), Obulco (Porcuna), Monda (Montilla), Ategua, Urso, Tuccis, Ulia, Asta, Nabrissa (Nebrija), Onoba (Huelva), Ossonoba (Lagos), as well as the mysterious Odysseia, in the hinterland of the Phoenician trading post of Abdera. Finally Castulo – 'the greatest town in Oretania', later an important centre of the Roman Tarraconensis – was situated to the south of Linares.

In spite of the late date of the evidence provided by Strabo – the first century B.C. – we must assume that these towns were founded prior to the Roman conquest.

Different types of town plan

It is often difficult to make out the plan of Iberian settlements since few of them have escaped the heavy erosion which affects steeply sloping ground in Spain. Very often the walls of houses have partly or wholly disappeared, leaving only traces of their foundations embedded in rocks which, formerly concealed by ancient buildings, have been uncovered by erosion and give a misleading idea of the lay-out today. Since the walls themselves are sometimes obliterated, one must be extremely cautious about reconstructing the plan of a town.

Successive occupations of the sites add to the difficulty. It is sometimes hard to distinguish the original plan (which may indeed be pre-Iberian) from the Roman plan (Azaila: plan, p. 83). The latter may have disappeared beneath the remains left by Visigoths or Arabs or even more recent inhabitants, as in the case of Saguntum, where the pre-Roman *oppidum* served as a stronghold right up to the nineteenth century.

The present state of research allows us to distinguish several typical plans. The most usual, and probably the oldest, is that of a village with a central street, varying in breadth, on either side of which are set out houses extending perpendicularly as far as the outer wall. This kind of plan is found at La Gesera (Teruel) and El Taratrato, where the walls of dwellings, reinforced on the south side, formed an almost continuous outer wall.

At San Antonio de Calaceite (Teruel) this was altered by the addition of an extension on a terrace below the level of the *oppidum*. At Azaila we can still make out the central street, despite the changes made during the Roman period. The case of Sant Juliá de Ramis is the most characteristic: the settlement is laid out lengthwise along a rocky crest several hundred metres in length, some houses being cut out of the rock. In any case the built-up area is generally adapted to the shape of the acropolis; at La Gesera the outer walls even follow the curve of the rock.

A kindred type of town plan, better suited to the contour of round or oval hilltops, is exemplified in Barranco Hondo (Mazaleón, Teruel), where the houses are distributed on either side of an irregular oblong central space.

At Olius the village is completely oval with an empty space in the centre and houses divided by party walls radiating towards the periphery. The type of dwelling in towns of this sort was characteristically an elongated rectangular construction, seven to ten metres long, comprising a single room or several rooms leading into one another.

As a rule the construction was a simple one: the foundations, 50 to 70 centimetres thick, were made of big stones laid down without mortar or joined together with earth. The walls were seldom of stone, but of large unbaked bricks (the Spanish *adobe*) piled flat on one another, or of tamped earth. Flat stones in the middle of the rooms and along the walls served as bases for the wooden posts that upheld the framework of the roof (Taratrato). Made of beaten and hardened clay, the floor was sometimes covered with a layer of pottery sherds which are of great value to the archaeologist. The roof had a single slope, running down to the façade which looked out on to the street, thus allowing rainwater to be collected.

The framework must have consisted merely of cross-beams, sometimes – though not always – with a central support. The houses were undoubtedly thatched. The use of the various rooms is suggested by the way they are furnished: the first, often quite small, may have been merely a vestibule (no. 8 in El Taratrato), but the presence of a side-door and a feeding-trough indicates that it may have served as a stable. Some rooms may even have been used for small livestock, others for cooking (house 5). The tiny chambers (2 × 2 metres) opening on to the outside may have been shops (house 9).

Public religious buildings are hard to identify. Cabré has discovered two temples of Iberian date at Azaila, at the western end of the town. One of these, close to the old gateway, is not noticeably different in lay-out from the dwellings. The other, which has disappeared, had been restored in Roman times, the interior being decorated with paintings of the so-called 'first style'.

Archaeologists have often looked for traces of public

buildings which could shed light on the political life of these settlements. At Azaila, as at San Antonio de Calaceite, large rooms have been found in the central houses, but this does not entitle one to draw any conclusion.

This type of town plan and of architecture appears, at the present stage of archaeological investigation, to be confined to the Aragonese region and to Catalonia. But one would not be surprised to find it elsewhere, considering the antiquity of its origin.

We know from discoveries made in the houses, that the lay-out with a central street goes back at least to the Hallstatt B-C period. The foundation of San Antonio de Calaceite can reasonably be dated about the beginning of the sixth century. The other *oppida* are contemporary or slightly later. The building techniques used, as well as the plans, are unquestionably of Celtic origin; their prototype has been found in Celtic settlements in the north of the Peninsula, at Cortes de Navarra, for example, where the first stratum goes back to the end of the Bronze Age or the beginning of the Iron Age (eighth century). Maluquer has even spoken of 'Celtic town plans' preceding Mediterranean-type plans in the Peninsula. But it is equally possible that the Celtic type of plan may itself have been influenced by the Mediterranean architecture of the end of the second millennium.

A second type of plan raises once again the problem of Mediterranean influences: it consists of what is virtually a regular grid of streets within a fairly concentrated perimeter, defined by a substantial wall. This is the case with Burriach (Cabrera de Mataró, Barcelona). This unusual town forms a large triangle, the tip of which clings to the crest of a hill, now occupied by a medieval *castillo*. The town was tiered in an amphitheatre on the hillside, looking south towards the sea, some 4 kilometres away as the crow flies. The pattern of the streets is less confused than at first appears, forming a network of diamond-shaped meshes which are well adapted to the terrain to avoid steeply sloping streets. The eastern wall still stands. Unfortunately no exhaustive excavation has yet been attempted on this exceptionally interesting site, which is threatened by coastal development.

The plan of Ullastret (which has so far not been explored) must be akin to that of Burriach. Other large towns like pre-Roman Tarragona, or Indika, were probably built on a chequer-board pattern. Certain villages of the Catalan coastal zone show signs of the same influence.

At Puig Castellar on the outskirts of Barcelona, which is at present being excavated, there seems not to have been a true grid. The area excavated on the western side has revealed three rather narrow streets running parallel. Here can be made out the plan of a number of houses somewhat different from those of the Aragon region. They consist of a single room, almost square, backed against the outer wall or extending between two streets. There is a greater use of stone here, always laid without mortar. The unbaked bricks are very small, like thinner versions of our modern bricks.

In the plan of these settlements, we can clearly trace the direct influence of Greece. Greek models were near by. At Ampurias (fig. 26) the native city Indika stood beside the Greek city (Nea Polis) which was enclosed within the same wall. Presumably the colonies of Rhode (Rosas), Hemero-skopeion (Denia), Mainaké and even the later trading posts of Alonis and Akra Leuké, small though they were, played an essential role. Except for Ampurias, these Greek settlements have left no notable traces of town planning. Like the Nea Polis itself, they were probably laid out on a regular plan with streets intersecting at right angles, according to the traditional pattern attributed to the celebrated Hippodamos of Miletus, which was freely interpreted throughout the Greek world.

The Iberians adapted this to the topography of their sites and the potential of local material. As for private dwellings, they were too simple to need models. We should note, however, that the Greek houses which can be discerned under the successive occupations of the Nea Polis of Ampurias were no less elementary.

A third group of habitation centres are perhaps the most typically indigenous or the most Iberian in the strict sense of the word. These are the hilltop towns, generally fortified like the rest. The houses form tiered terraces over the side of the hill or the acropolis, often facing the same way but unevenly laid out, so that the streets – when one can recognise them – or the lanes between houses, form a zigzag pattern.

This apparently untidy plan is widespread in the Iberian north-east and in the region of Valencia, where dozens of examples have been located. It certainly extends into Upper Andalusia and possibly even into the Tartessian region. The best known examples are El Puig (Alcoy, Alicante), El Cabezo de Tio Pio (Archena, Murcia), Meca (Alpera, Albacete), San Miguel de Liria (Valencia) and above all La Bastida de les Alcuses (Mogente, Valencia).

Finally the acropolis of Despeñaperros (Jaén) belongs to the same category. Situated on the way from the Valencian region to Alicante, the Iberian town of La Bastida stretches from east to west over an 800-metre-long hill, covering its crest and northern flank. It is of particular interest since, having been occupied from the fifth to the end of the third centuries, it was abandoned at the time of the Roman conquest. It is not easy to reconstruct the houses which appear to comprise a set of three or four square or oblong rooms. One can sometimes recognise a kitchen, a cellar, and a weaver's workroom. The walls are made of stones and *adobe* bricks according to the traditional design, and fortunately one of these bricks has been found intact. It was made of clay mixed with straw and measured no less than $35 \times 25 \times 12$ centimetres. The floor of beaten earth was sometimes laid with stones or even flagged. The roof was undoubtedly of thatch upheld by posts fixed in the centre of the rooms.

In spite of the indigenous character of a town like La Bastida, Greek influence is unquestionably recognisable in the way the walls are orientated and in the eastern entrance which widens out in the axis of the town. Contacts with Greece were frequent, moreover, as is evident from the abundance of Greek pottery discovered in these dwellings, mingled with specimens of native art.

Fortifications

One of the most interesting chapters in Iberian art is that of the protective walls surrounding habitation centres, of which they are sometimes the sole remains and which are often of undeniable architectural value. Moreover, they raise intriguing archaeological problems of chronology and influence.

The masonry of these walls varies considerably in character and, surprisingly enough, a single wall sometimes contains a variety of stonework. In such cases different periods of construction have been postulated, but occasionally there has merely been reparation.

The oldest method of construction adopted by the Iberians, probably from Greek models, is the 'cyclopean' wall. Large blocks of stone laid flat, measuring 1 to 3 metres in length and weighing up to 10 tons (notably the monolithic lintels) are wedged together by means of stones lodged in the joints, which are filled with earth.

Cyclopean masonry is still visible in part of the surrounding wall of the Nea Polis of Ampurias, though it has been greatly reworked. This may be the Peninsular prototype of a style dating from the end of the sixth century. But considering how widespread it is throughout the Iberian area, it could be a traditional pattern remembered from the Megalithic period (the Bronze Age). It exists in such sites as Ullastret, Burriach, Castell de la Fosca and Tivisa, where part of the surrounding walls are built in this fashion, and at Carmona

and even at Despeñaperros, where a massive section still survives in the southern part of the wall.

But the most conspicuous example, and the one whose date is the most uncertain, is at Tarragona. The cyclopean wall encircles the old town and traces of it are visible right up to the market place in the centre of the new town. In the eastern area, near the Puerta de San Magín, a section about 7 metres high is still standing. Elsewhere it serves as the base for the Roman wall which is constructed of isodomous stones. Here there are enormous blocks of stone, especially around the small doors (fig. 28) which must have been subsidiary entrances. Every sort of date has been suggested for this wall, from the Mycenean period (thirteenth century B.C.) to the Roman occupation. Today it is generally assumed to

28 Opposite: *Tarragona. The San Antonio gate in the 'cyclopean' wall. Aperture approximately 2·1 by 1·50 metres*

29 Below: *Olérdola (Barcelona). The surrounding wall showing pseudo-polygonal masonry.*

be of relatively late date – the third or second century B.C.

Other Iberian walls reveal contrasting types of masonry. The commonest – that which I shall christen pseudo-isodomous – is composed of large blocks cut in rough parallele-pipeds and laid in almost regular courses with a few small stones set in the jointing to correct the unevenness. This style was widely employed at Ibros, at Burriach and even at Ampurias in the southern wall of the native and Greek town. At Saguntum it can be traced behind later work of the Roman period.

Closely akin to this style (and sometimes used immediately after it) is a kind of masonry that should be described as 'pseudo-polygonal' – blocks cut to fit together, but without much attempt to maintain a constant level within each course. So popular was this stonework among Spaniards at all periods since the fourth century B.C. that one is tempted to call it *opus hispanicus*. It prevails in places as diverse as Ampurias, La Torre de Foyos (Lucena del Cid, Castellón), and Torre Seca (Casinos, Valencia), the best example being unquestionably Olérdola (Barcelona) (fig. 29). It was applied to the lower part of the walls built at the beginning of the second century B.C., the upper courses having been subject to constant refashioning until recent times.

The Greek origin of these two categories of masonry is clearly evident. One must also mention a rustic kind of native stonework based on small irregular blocks wedged together with earth and pebbles (which is also common throughout the Peninsula) at Puig Castellar, San Antonio de Calaceite, Tivisa, Despeñaperros, Osuna and elsewhere. Such stonework was generally only used for the facing. The interior of the walls, which were some 3 to 6 metres thick, was filled with stones and earth piled haphazardly. Today it is difficult to comprehend what these walls were like at their full height. In many instances stone appeared only in the lower part. At Ullastret and at Tivissa the upper area of the wall was definitely made of unbaked bricks or rammed earth. This technique obviously simplified the work of construction. Actually the walls of Iberian towns must have resembled those of Marrakesh or Tlemcen.

As a rule, walls followed the natural contour of the terrain. They might crown a hilltop, as at La Bastida or San Antonio de Calaceite or cling just below its summit, enclosing the town on the hillside (Burriach). If the site was sufficiently inaccessible, walls were built only on the lower side of the town on either side of the entrance as at Olérdola, where huge cliffs surrounded the *oppidum* on three sides (fig. 30). Sometimes buildings are to be seen outside the wall: dwellings (Saguntum), or wells (Olérdola), or grain silos later used as refuse dumps (Burriach), but the greater part of architectural remains are naturally *intra muros*.

Occasionally the walls were enlarged to take in a new district (San Antonio de Calaceite) or doubled (Puig Castellar). Supplementary enclosures are also found, as at La Bastida, and must have served as shelter for men and animals from the neighbouring countryside in the event of attack.

The line of the surrounding wall is sometimes broken by square or round towers, or both (as at Ullastret), built usually in the same fashion as the walls. The entrances to towns and villages emulated Greek models. At Ullastret the main gate was protected on the right – the vulnerable side, since the assailant would carry his shield on the left – by a square projecting bastion surmounted by a round tower. This is repeated at Olérdola. At Tivisa the gate is defended on either side by two massive bastions standing at an acute angle, a device worthy of Vauban.

Some hills were surmounted by small isolated strongholds for garrisons, as at Cellecs, where a trapezium of 50×80 metres is divided in two by a double inner wall. At the fortress of Rochina (Sot de Ferrer, Castellón) a double row of small rooms runs for 35 metres on either side of a central lane. The ramparts are simply the reinforced outside walls of these rooms.

A special note must be made of the isolated towers, or *atalayas*, which have been an aspect of the Spanish Mediterranean landscape since the Bronze Age. The Iberians built or restored many of these, such as the magnificent Torre de Foyos which guarded the way between the plain of Castellón and the region of Teruel. This *atalaya*, 15×11 metres in area, was elliptical in shape. Two concentric walls, still standing over three metres high, are separated by a narrow paved passage. A zigzagging entry, leading to an oval room 6×3 metres, prompts the query whether the handful of men holding this fortress could have defended it effectively. Presumably a construction of this sort must have been combined with a system of defences which has long since vanished.

Sanctuaries

Our knowledge of the architecture of Iberian sanctuaries has been hindered by the lack of archaeological prospecting in the south of the Peninsula, and also by the destruction of valuable remains discovered during excavation in the early years of this century.

The cave sanctuaries of Andalusia, in Oretanian territory, have naturally stood up better to the ravages of time. At Castellar de Santisteban, for instance, the caves are still intact and the walls, which have been buried again since the excavations I undertook there in 1966 and 1968, are also preserved.

Unfortunately this is not the case at Despeñaperros, one of the most impressive centres of Iberian religion and art. The

30 Olérdola (Barcelona). North-eastern spur of the oppidum

sense of awe and mystery that pervades it strikes the least sensitive visitor. The red cliff of the acropolis, cleft by the yawning mouth of the cavern, is visible from afar on the road from Andalusia to Madrid, even before one reaches the narrow pass of Despeñaperros that cuts across it to the west. This is the historic boundary between Andalusia and Castile, the spot where European and southern influences mingle.

Even if it did not constitute a clear ethnic demarcation in antiquity, it seems to have been a junction between the domains of the Celts, the Tartessians and the peoples of the south-east. The sanctuary established at the foot of its acropolis must have been visited by all the peoples of ancient Spain. Today the buildings surrounding the cavern have been completely destroyed. Cabré has made out two successive temples on a terrace supported by a low wall; the older of these consisted of a rectangular room oriented east to west. This was held to belong to the fifth century and to have been the oldest known Iberian centre of worship.

It is unfortunately impossible to reconstruct it. The orientation and shape of the building suggest Greek influence. On a level with the sanctuary, the ancient road which was Iberian, Punic and Roman in turn, and which was the main road to Madrid until the eighteenth century, runs through the almost obliterated remains of the surrounding wall (plan, p. 84). Only a gateway and a few cyclopean blocks have survived. After a couple of bends, the road re-emerged through the wall by another gate, which Cabré found, but which I have been unable to identify. Within this enclosure lay a vast area, some 40 hectares, in which there is no trace of the site of any town. Cabré suggested a sacred grove connected with the sanctuary's two springs and the Collado de los Jardines (the Hillside of the Gardens). At one time I put forward the hypothesis of a *temenos*, an area dedicated to the god of the place. Actually it may have been a sacred enclosure in which pilgrims gathered on ceremonial occasions, or simply a place of refuge.

The sanctuaries of the south-east and the Spanish Levant are quite different. We have already mentioned the 'temples' of Azaila, and these must be considered as the only known urban sanctuaries. Elsewhere sanctuaries seem to have been outside towns. Quantities of votive offerings, for example, have been found at Cigarralejo, in an ill-defined group of buildings which may have been a village. The sanctuary of La Luz – now almost destroyed by modern building – must have been laid out in somewhat the same way, but it was not far from the urban complex of Verdolay. In any case, cave sanctuaries may have existed in Iberian times in the Levant and the south-east, as is suggested by the votive grotto of La Albufereta.

An Iberian temple (or treasure house?) has been found at El Cerro de los Santos (Montealegre, Albacete). On a hill (the *cerro*, which owes its name to the countless votive offerings of stone, the *santos*) there still existed at the end of the last century the remains of an edifice which was promptly recorded in 1871 by the archaeologist Savirón, who was sent for from Madrid after the discovery of the statues.

A. García y Bellido has suggested that it may have been a Roman temple, and it may belong to the second century B.C. The plan is a simple one: an entrance to the east, with the foot of a staircase and an elongated *cella*, the whole construction measuring about 15 × 10 metres. But this is only a foundation plan, and it is impossible to reconstruct either the elevation or even the plan of the *cella*, which stood well above ground level. Pierre Paris has suggested the idea of a temple *in antis*. Perhaps it belonged to the Ionic order, as is implied by a fragment of a volute discovered nearby on the hillside.

Tombs

The Iberians cremated their dead. They practised various forms of burial, varying according to period and region but chiefly according to the affluence of the deceased. We shall consider here only those tombs having an architectural character.

One of the earliest noteworthy types of tomb was the tumulus in which a small chamber contained the cist holding the ashes, surrounded by items customarily left in the grave. This was in common practice from the Bronze Age onwards. The base of the tumulus might consist of a round or square stone floor on which stood the funerary urn, as at El Cigarralejo. More elaborate were the tumuli of Galera, consisting of an entrance passage and a square chamber, sometimes with a prop in the centre. The walls were of dressed or undressed stone, the roof of large flagstones carefully laid together. Among tombs of this category, one, which may have been a prince's, is of immensely careful workmanship. A door with a false arch opened on to a low passage leading to a square chamber. The capital of the central pillar was remarkable, being a sort of double corbel decorated with

31 Los Alcazares (Murcia). Capital from a column. Length 51 cm. (Provincial Archaeological Museum, Murcia)

volutes and beads, freely inspired by the Ionic order. The whole tomb belongs to the fourth century.

Far more spectacular are the *hypogea* of Toya (the ancient Tugia). The most extraordinary of these, excavated by Cabré in 1921, is a tomb consisting of three chambers of 5 × 5 metres, entirely built of large limestone blocks in pseudo-polygonal masonry. The central and southern chambers are constructed with particular care, with benches running round the walls and shelves upheld by stone corbels. Above the shelves are niches intended for urns. To relieve the monolithic lintels, the piers of the doors are curved back oddly above the passage. The roof is made of large flat flagstones.

In contrast with this fine construction, the decoration is somewhat meagre: the angles of the shelves are merely chamfered, and the cornices of the central and southern chambers display no more than a shallow concave moulding. The items in the grave enable us to assess the date of the

32 La Alcudia (Elche, Alicante). Votive altar made in limestone. Length 8·5 cm.

tomb – the end of the fourth century. This class of tomb is uncommon, even in Spain (examples are known only at Baza and at Almedinilla), and it clearly reflects certain Etruscan *hypogea* (the tomb with capitals at Cerveteri) and particularly Ionian ones. Its architectural form has probably been adapted from these.

Architectural ornament

Many elements of architectural decoration have been discovered during excavation, though unfortunately seldom *in situ*. In particular, Iberian artists were inspired by the monuments built in their colonies by the Greeks and later by the Romans. They reproduced with a greater or lesser degree of fidelity the Classical orders, notably the Ionic or Corinthian, the beauty of which attracted them (fig. 31). Thus we find a profusion of ovolos, olives, coin-mouldings, scrolls, volutes, vitruvian scrolls and braids.

On a fragment of a capital at El Llano de la Consolación (Albacete), the sculptor has set a line of pearls and coin-mouldings under the abacus. The bell of the capital itself is made up of large ovolos, while the angles are decorated with standing volutes which recall the Corinthian order.

The Ionic order was often faithfully imitated, as at El Cerro de los Santos. At Baeza, on the other hand, an 'Ionic' capital has been found where volutes are completely crushed by a massive abacus. The Louvre once owned a block of stone from Osuna decorated with bas-reliefs: a fluted column with an 'aeolic' capital between two bands adorned with braids. A small votive altar from Elche owes nothing to the Ionic order but its denticulation (fig. 32).

Of much greater interest, however, are the original creations developed from motifs borrowed from minor *objets d'art*, whether Greek, Oriental or indigenous, particularly jewellery and vases, combined with a few details borrowed from the Classical orders. If we add to this a certain Celtic influence, recognisable in the geometrical patterns, we shall realise the wide variety of Iberian architectural decoration.

New forms were thus created, such as the serpentine volute at Galera which we have already mentioned. We meet another version of this at Montilla combined with braids and ovolos and on one at Elche where the volutes are intertwined. A new motif, which must be interpreted as a palmette inscribed within a mandorla, adorns the capital of a pilaster at Elche. This is a free transposition of the motif of the 'cloeds palmette' found in some of the jewellery from Aliseda.

Even more surprising are the pieces that include Celtic elements. The museum at Ampurias owns a door-jamb decorated with a spiral frieze which suggests Greek archaic art, together with a broad band patterned with waves ending in volutes and swastikas. Finally a small votive altar shaped like a capital bears at its angles faces recalling the severed heads from the Celto-Ligurian sanctuaries of southern France (fig. 33).

*33 Castella de Santisteban (Jaén). Votive
altar made of limestone. Height 12 cm.*
(Archaeological Museum, Barcelona)

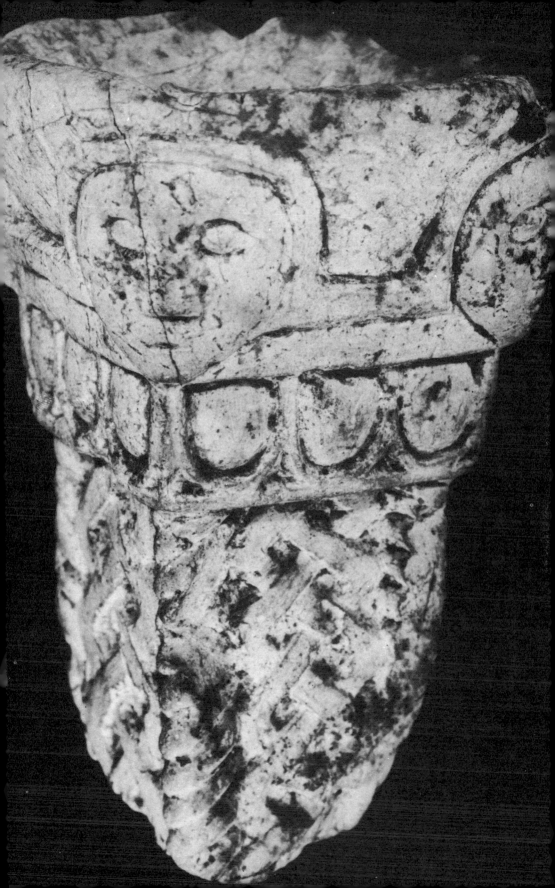

CHAPTER 6
Sculpture: the creative genius of Iberia

When, in December 1897, the Dama de Elche, recently acquired by Pierre Paris, was exhibited in the Salle de l'Apadana in the Louvre, most archaeologists and the French public were suddenly made aware that a new province of ancient art – virtually unknown hitherto – had been dazzlingly revealed. People began to talk about Iberian art, giving it a wider meaning than we do today, since the term Iberian then covered the whole of pre-Roman art in Spain.

Certain pieces, as we have seen, had already attracted the attention of Spanish and foreign archaeologists, but the general public, for lack of knowledge, had remained un-affected. Moreover, the pieces known at that time – a handful of bronzes from the Sierra Morena and a few objects from the Cerro de los Santos – had been relegated to the category of 'barbarian' art, at that period considered unimportant or at any rate devoid of aesthetic value.

And now surprisingly Paris was confronted with a Spanish statue which was 'good art', and thanks to which it would prove possible to establish parallels with Classical or Oriental sculpture. Iberian art, and Iberian sculpture in particular, had emerged from obscurity. In the wake of the great Dama the various achievements of Iberian art, hitherto neglected, were gradually (and until 1914 somewhat hesitantly) revealed.

It did not happen at once. We have seen with what con-tempt Pierre Paris treated the Iberian bronzes in his *Essai*

Sculpture: the creative genius of Iberia

of 1902–1903. His successors were more indulgent, even enthusiastic: R. Lantier for instance, following the dedicated Director of the Madrid museum, J.-R. Mélida, pointed out the archaeological and historical, as well as the aesthetic interest of Iberian sculpture.

Today, when scientific questions are no longer affected by aesthetic considerations, the rejection of 'barbarian' or primitive art appears peculiarly outmoded. This change in attitude enables us to judge them more freely.

Aesthetic judgements, in which contemporary archaeologists seldom indulge, are particularly hard to formulate in the case of Iberian sculpture. It does not make the same immediate appeal as Egyptian sculpture, for instance, or the Greek or Roman sculpture with which we are more familiar. More often than not the visitor to the Madrid museum sees only a series of big stones representing animals or hieratic human figures, a host of tiny bronzes, too small – a few centimetres high – to attract one's attention, and a set of terracotta figurines that seem coarsely and clumsily modelled. An approach to Iberian art must necessarily be accompanied by a searching examination. One must gradually become familiar with its forms, its unfamiliar volumes, the crude workmanship of some pieces and the exaggeratedly delicate elaboration of others. Photography and drawings provide valuable help in one's discovery.

For Iberian sculpture is an art of detail, as is much primitive sculpture. Often the artist has treated only a single feature, neglecting the rest of the figure, which does not interest him. A man may be reduced to a face, a hand, an offering. That one can understand easily enough. But the more complex and elaborate works are in fact subject to the same limitations; here details are multiplied and juxtaposed, yet the artist has not sought, or has been unable to achieve, any real balance or general harmony.

The problem of the competence or incompetence of Iberian artists seems meaningless. Iberian sculptures often

eveal surprising skill, deft craftsmanship, and a meticulous
are for detail. Pierre Paris noted this, though he was not the
rst to do so. How does it happen in that case, he wondered,
1at certain arms are too short, certain hands too big, some
odies spool-shaped, some heads merely spherical shapes?
'he realistic representation of a perfectly proportioned
gure was probably never attempted by Iberian artists, who
imed at something quite different. The development of
berian sculpture never led it towards Classicism for the
ime reason. It is inevitably futile to judge Iberian art with
eference to Classical criteria.

Nevertheless, paradoxical though this may seem, a know-
dge of archaic and Classical art is indispensable for the
nderstanding of Iberian art. It enables one to assess not
nly the difference but also the connection between them,
nce the first achievements of Iberian art were based on the
rt of Greece and the East. As with architecture, we have to
now what the Iberians borrowed and adopted, what they
ansformed, what they neglected and finally what they
eated with the aid of their native genius, flowering in the
roximity of the fertile Mediterranean.

It must be said at once that the art historian will find more
) interest him in their indigenous creations than in their
orrowings. When he has become familiar with them (which
1ay take a little time), he will acknowledge the extraordinary
xpressive vigour of these figures. Then he will realise that the
rtist has succeeded in simplifying and schematising contours
nd volumes so as to achieve a kind of spatial geometry,
ringing almost all these pieces to the verge of abstract art.
Ve cannot fail today to ascribe creative genius of this sort to
itochthonous Iberian art.

But Iberian sculpture is important not only on aesthetic
ounds. It is one of the surest means, in the absence of
early decipherable texts, of understanding Iberian civilisa-
on. We know the difficulties encountered by the archaeol-
zist seeking to reconstitute the origins of the Iberian people,

Sculpture: the creative genius of Iberia

of whose ethnic characteristics we know little if anything
Sculpture provides us with thousands of images of thes
Iberians who have left us so little information about them
selves. It is possible to attempt to reconstruct a physical, or a
any rate a facial type, by studying this vast number of figure

We are on even surer ground when we seek to reconstruc
at least in part, the social hierarchy of the Iberians by mear
of the representation of social types in sculpture and i
pottery. And the precise rendering of detail in dress an
adornment means that we know as much today about th
dress of the Iberians as about that of the Greeks, althoug
we are still ignorant of the names of the various items.

Finally, what clearer evidence could we have about th
primitive religion of the Iberians than is provided by thes
statues? They are all, or almost all, votive offerings, repr
senting the donor in an attitude of prayer, presentatior
libation or sacred dance. Here as elsewhere, archaeolog
provides the surest source for the historian.

Iberian archaism in the seventh and sixth centuries B.C.
The most primitive examples of art in Spain are extremel
scarce. From the third millennium we have a number of
engraved plaques of schist, a few clay or stone figurin
representing the 'mother goddess', to use the traditional tern
Later, in the middle of the Bronze Age, sculpture becom
even rarer, and only a few sketchy reliefs are found, apa
from the material already mentioned. Although these objec
lack any definite form, they have often been attributed t
hypothetical Oriental models. The meagreness of plastic a:
at this period is the more surprising in view of the incon
parable wealth of second millenary sculpture around th
Aegean Sea and in the East.

In fact the earliest Spanish sculptures were the direct resu
of Oriental art. We have seen how the Phoenicians settle
first at Gadir, then, by gradual escalation, spread along th
southern coast of Spain, from Málaga to Almeria (Torre d

Mar, Almuñecar) between the eleventh century B.C. (if we accept the traditional date of the founding of Gadir) and the eighth. It is likely that these active traders brought in a certain number of luxury articles (for instance, carved ivories and jewellery) and statuettes which were quickly copied by local artists, whether natives or immigrants.

A few years ago many objects, particularly ivories and jewels, were thought to be imported articles. It has now been realised that there are considerable differences between these objects and those which are authentically Oriental and which are usually much more delicate and more finely worked. Thus in the case of the ivories, A. Blanco has shown that the oldest specimens, decorated with figures of deer and fantastic animals, were in fact made by immigrant artists at the beginning of the seventh century. In this instance the imported prototype is missing.

On the other hand we have a few very fine examples of small imported Oriental sculptures. Paradoxically they have all (or almost all) been found far from the coastal trading posts, in the valley of the Guadalquivir or in Upper Andalusia in the interior of the Tartessian region. Perhaps this may be explained by the inadequate excavation hitherto made on such sites as Cadiz (Gadir) and the partial destruction of the coastal settlements, of which quite often only the necropolei remain. The other no less surprising characteristic of these pieces, is that they are almost all exceptional: few of them belong to familiar Eastern series.

The most ancient is probably the celebrated 'priest of Cadiz' (fig. 34). When the foundations of the town's telephone exchange were being dug in 1928, a workman's pickaxe encountered a statuette 5 metres down; this in itself implies a very early date in that zone in the centre of the original town. This small bronze, 13 centimetres high, its face covered with a gold mask, immediately aroused much controversy as to its date and derivation. Today the tendency is to ascribe it to the ninth century B.C. and to consider it as of Phoenician

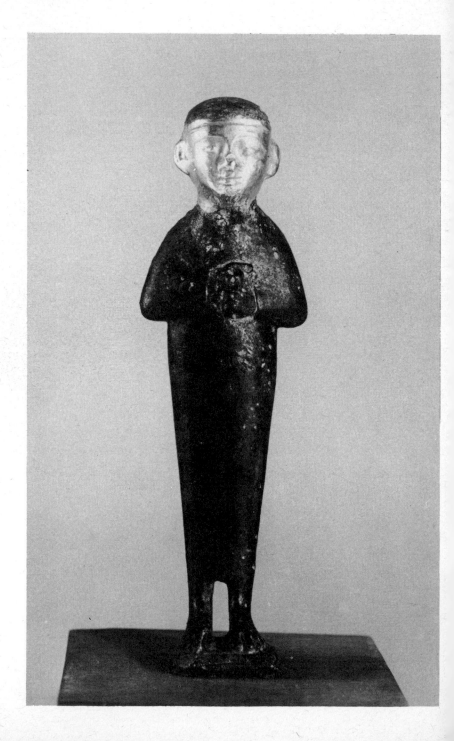

34 Cadiz. Bronze statuette of priest with gold mask. Height 13 cm. (National Archaeological Museum, Madrid)

or Egyptian workmanship. Yet one would search in vain for an Iberian statuette directly influenced by this bronze, still less a local copy. Such lucky finds are rare in archaeology. In any case we have here proof of the presence of Eastern plastic art in Iberia.

It is not the only one: we possess some Phoenician statuettes of Baal which are of Spanish origin, although one cannot be more specific, and in particular a fine nude statuette of Astarte found in the neighbourhood of Seville, recognisable from the generous curves of her figure and above all from the Phoenician dedication on the base, which proves the existence of an Eastern Semitic community in Spain in the seventh century B.C.

More famous than the priest of Cadiz or the Astarte of Seville is the goddess discovered in a tomb at Galera in the heart of Andalusia. This alabaster statuette, measuring only 18 centimetres high, represents a goddess seated on a throne between two sphinxes. The great tasselled wig, the robe with its embroidered trimming, the necklaces and the sphinxes' wings are rendered with a remarkable delicacy, such as we encounter later in Iberian bronzes (fig. 18). The peculiar feature of this figure, which enables us to identify her as the goddess of fertility (the 'mistress of animals'), is that she holds on her knees a bowl to receive the liquid offering which was poured in through the head and gushed out through holes in the chest. Opinions differ as to the origin of the statuette, which may be Syrian or Phoenician, but its workmanship suggests a seventh-century date.

Apart from these purely Oriental objects which formed the basis of Ibero-Tartessian art, a second category of Oriental pieces made in Spain has been recognised. Such for instance are the bronze plaques decorating a cauldron which was found at Castulo in the heart of the Oretanian region and which represent a clothed figure of Astarte holding a lotus flower, her hair dressed in the manner of the Egyptian Hathor, with ringlets hanging over her ears. A. Blanco ascribes a sixth-century date to them. We thus have proof that the earliest influence which left its mark on Iberian plastic art in the seventh century, or indeed which may have given rise to it, was that of the East. This influence spread northwards through Spain, if we take as a starting-point the trading posts of the Costa del Sol, towards Upper Andalusia or from the south-west to the north-east if we see it as originating in the region of Cadiz and the mythical town of Tartessos and spreading along the valley of the Guadalquivir. These Eastern influences, which are at the source of Ibero-Tartessian art, spread far beyond Andalusia into Estremadura and Castile, as is confirmed by the bronze utensils to be considered later.

But were these Eastern influences the only ones to serve as models to the artists who were learning to practise sculpture in the seventh century? Small-scale Greek sculptures may have played their part in the Tartessian zone at the same period or a little later. We know that Phoenician navigators brought in Greek objects such as those 'proto-corinthian' vases which have been found in the necropolis of Almuñecar. The Phoenicians, however, did not have the exclusive monopoly of trade in this region. Greeks from Chalkis and Rhodes, Samians (the voyage of Kolaios was about 650 B.C.) may also have brought in objects such as the famous helmet of Jerez, which belongs to the seventh century, or the sixth-century bronze *oenochoe* from Granada. Eastern iconographical themes, at a time when Greek art was subject to Oriental influence, may naturally have been passed on through Greek intermediaries.

It is hard today to distinguish between the two influences. One example will show this clearly: that of the great warrior of Medina de las Torres (Badajoz). This figure, 34 centimetres high, is the largest known Iberian bronze and is now in the British Museum. It represents a standing warrior wearing a short tunic, his left leg forward and presumably brandishing two lances. While his tunic is definitely of Eastern type,

Egyptian influence is recognisable in the shinbone of the massive legs. It is also found, however, in Greek statues of the same period. This is also true of the hairstyle and the full, almond-eyed face, in which J.-M. Blázquez has seen Samian characteristics. Now Samian plastic art at this period – the beginning of the sixth century B.C. – displays marked Asiatic influences. Obviously any attempt at precision in this field is doomed to failure.

Oretanian bronzes

Graeco-Asiatic influences, spreading northwards, thus reached the upper valley of the Guadalquivir and the mountainous zone of the Sierra Morena, corresponding to the Oretania of antiquity. In the course of the sixth century, owing no doubt to Phocean colonisation in south-eastern Spain, Greek influence took another route, east to west this time, starting from the trading posts on the coast of the Spanish Levant and going up into the hinterland by way of the great plateaux of the Júcar and the Segura region. They thus reached Upper Andalusia, that natural junction which ensured contact between Iberians and Celts.

It was at Despeñaperros, in the heart of this region, that from the early sixth century onwards there developed a flourishing school of bronze-workers, which was to endure through all the vicissitudes of history until the fourth century A.D., when the triumph of Christianity brought about the closing of pagan sanctuaries. During the course of a thousand years pilgrims must have deposited there hundreds of thousands of votive offerings, which the priests threw down on the hillside when the cave itself and the terrace of the temple were over-full. At the foot of the terrace alone, thousands have been discovered. Unauthorised excavators have found others in the cracks of the rock or in the dry bed of the stream, eroded to mere lumps of corroded metal. Presumably the whole collection represents only a tiny part of what was offered to the local deity.

Sculpture: the creative genius of Iberia

The second centre of production, at Castellar de Santiste-ban, which probably began towards the end of the sixth century, was somewhat south-east of this, along the route from Linares to Albacete, running alongside the ancient road from Castulo to Libisosa. Like Despeñaperros this is a rock sanctuary, but the site, though more welcoming, is lacking in grandeur. There are five grottoes ranged at the foot of a cliff overlooking a cornfield bordered by fig-trees, in the midst of which the spring of the sanctuary has been found. Thousands of votive offerings have been picked up in this field but few of them belong to the archaic period with which we are concerned. This sanctuary no doubt continued to function as long as that of Despeñaperros. It must be stressed that these two centres unquestionably produced more than nine-tenths of all known Iberian bronzes.

These bronzes must have been made *in situ*, for tools and crucibles have been discovered not far from the sanctuaries. The supply of metal was easily secured since there were copper mines in the vicinity, as well as lead mines. Only tin came from afar: from the Cassiterides islands north-west of Spain, or from western Cornwall in Britain.

The manufacturing process applied (which had come from Greece or from Asia), was that of *cire perdue* casting. Although simpler than the hollow casting method, it had the disadvantage of using more metal and thus confining the artist to the production of small-scale objects, measuring 4 to 10 centimetres for the most part. When the metal had cooled the mould was broken and the cast, more or less successful according to the quality of the metal and the degree of distortion undergone during cooling, was retouched by filing, scraping and polishing. Flaws, blisters, excrescences in the metal or a granular surface made such retouching necessary, and it could moreover give an incomparable finish to the work, especially on archaic pieces. The engraver often traced with his burin certain physical details: the contour of the eye, the slit of the mouth, the hair or else the folds of the garment.

Special chisels with hollow points left small rings on the bronze which served to denote eyes, breasts, ankles and the patterned edges of robes and cloaks on the more elaborate statuettes.

Towards the end of the fifth century, it is believed, artists began to produce more schematic figures with the aid of a metal rod, cast and then divided into pieces which were hammered and then summarily engraved. Votive offerings of this type eventually became by far the most numerous. The archaic period undoubtedly produced the finest and most interesting pieces.

Little is known about the birth of bronze sculpture in Oretania. It would be interesting to learn, as a reliably dated discovery may enable us to do some day, what the earliest statuettes were like. Were they rudimentary figures, like those of proto-geometric Greek art, or real works of art by artists who had learnt directly from foreigners? I am inclined to opt for the former hypothesis, but with no absolute certainty, since rudimentary figures were produced in Iberia at all periods, and are often the result of the degeneration of a type too often repeated.

For instance, certain nude figurines are unquestionably archaic. They may even have been the earliest creations of primitive artists in bronze; see for example the worshipper from Despeñaperros now in the Municipal Museum at Valencia, raising his head beseechingly towards his god, his great hands lying flat against his thighs (fig. 35). The elongation of head and neck, the slenderness of the trunk contrasted with the breadth of the shoulders, suggest the influence of those 'daedalic' sculptures which were made in the Dorian regions of Greece in the seventh century.

Another piece in the same museum, the figure of a woman, found at Sabiote not far from Castellar, may perhaps be contemporary with this (fig. 36). Here the proportions of the figure are less definite, but the finish is better: the rough marks made by the file, as seen on the companion piece, have been eliminated by the scraper. Here again the artist has stressed the sexual characteristics, the attitude of prayer, and the expression of the face, open-mouthed as though in supplication.

A considerable degree of craftsmanship was already required to fashion such little masterpieces of only 8 centimetres high. It needed even greater skill to create the more elaborate archaic types, the sources of which are more clearly recognisable. Thus we find a first series connected with daedalic statuary from which it borrows the triangular elongated face, the ridge of the eye-socket prolonging the bridge of the nose, eyes rimmed with prominent lids, and ears like double volutes. These characteristics are obviously less clearly marked than in Greece (fig. 15).

The series includes both male and female figures with

almost identical proportions. Only their garments differ. The men wear short tunics, with pointed necklines, tightly belted at the waist. Round their chests they sometimes wear threefold or fourfold cords, the significance of which is obscure. The legs are treated in the manner of Eastern and Greek bronzes, particularly the protuberances at knee level; an example being the figure from the Vich museum (Gerona) offering his god two flat objects which may be loaves or cakes (pl. IIIb). The women are dressed in long robes, such as the men also wear at times, and on their heads they have flat mitres or neatly plaited wigs, ending in two braids hanging down over their breasts. A figurine in the Madrid museum (fig. 37) is of this type, although somewhat later than those previously mentioned.

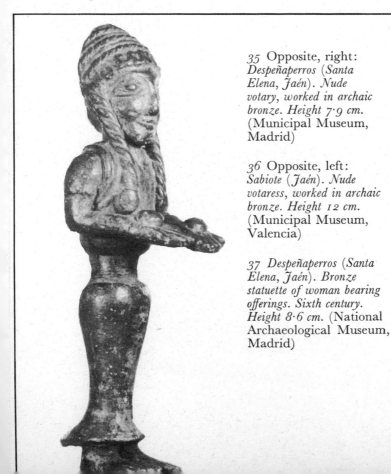

35 Opposite, right: *Despeñaperros (Santa Elena, Jaén). Nude votary, worked in archaic bronze. Height 7·9 cm.* (Municipal Museum, Madrid)

36 Opposite, left: *Sabiote (Jaén). Nude votaress, worked in archaic bronze. Height 12 cm.* (Municipal Museum, Valencia)

37 Despeñaperros (Santa Elena, Jaén). Bronze statuette of woman bearing offerings. Sixth century. Height 8·6 cm. (National Archaeological Museum, Madrid)

Sculpture: the creative genius of Iberia

This figure, moreover, suggests an influence which was to be strongly evident in the middle of the sixth century: that of eastern Greece or Ionia, whose navigators frequented the shores of Spain. A statuette from the Madrid museum (fig. 7) would appear, did it not wear the Iberian priestly mantle, to have come straight from Greece or from Etruria, which was then undergoing the same influence. The elongated face betrays a hint of a smile and the profile, the curve of the nose, the full lips, the heavy chin and the waving locks are all closely related to their models (fig. 38).

Samian influence sometimes resulted in a certain heaviness in the treatment of the face, as in the austere countenance of the Dama, who is closely enveloped in her great veil (fig.39). Her round mitre, the magnificence of the veil, her train and her necklace with its great *bullae* indicate a lady of high rank. The influence of the East is visible in the peculiar treatment of the hands. It is even more evident in the series of 'priests' and 'priestesses'.

38 Opposite: *Despeñaperros (Santa Elena, Jaén). Detail from a bronze statuette of a votary. Sixth century. Overall height 10 cm.* (National Archaeological Museum, Madrid)

39 *Despeñaperros (Santa Elena, Jaén). Bronze statuette of votaress. Sixth century. Height 11·2 cm.* (National Archaeological Museum, Madrid)

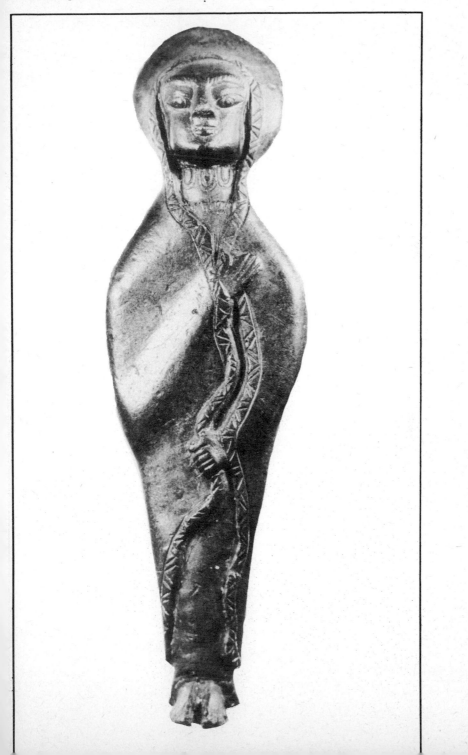

Sculpture: the creative genius of Iberia

These interesting figurines have puzzled archaeologists. Their tonsured heads, the veils that sometimes cover their heads and shoulders, their flounced robes edged with braid have caused them to be identified as the priests of ancient Iberia, or at least as those of the sanctuaries of Despeñaperros and Castellar, since no specimens have been found elsewhere (fig. 11). The priestesses wear a low mitre and their hair is worn *en bandeaux*. Otherwise their dress is identical with that of the priests and so are their great necklaces with amulet-containers, real specimens of which we shall discuss later. They

40 Despeñaperros (Santa Elena, Jaén). Bronze horse. Sixth century. Length 10·4 cm. (National Archaeological Museum, Madrid)

have the same faces with flat cheeks, thin lips and large semi-circular eyes. Even stranger is the similarity in the modelling of their bodies. The priestess's bosom is suggested by a slight swelling under the thin stuff of her garment (presumably fine lawn), but the curve of the belly, the short thighs and the large pyramidal feet are the same for both sexes. The Eastern origin is very obvious (fig. 12).

This account of Iberian archaic statuettes would not be complete without a mention of the tiny but remarkable figures of horsemen. One of the earliest, made by the bronze-workers of Despeñaperros, is certainly the statuette in the Madrid museum (fig. 5). This depicts a man leaning back-wards, holding his horse back as he presents two lances to the god, with his small round buckler slung over his back. The archaic Greek character is evident in the slenderness of the horse, which recurs in certain contemporary examples from Despeñaperros (fig. 40), and of the rider, whose broad-calved legs recall the figures on coins. The shape of the head, however, is Ibero-Semitic.

Of much later date, in fact one of the last specimens of Iberian archaic art, is the famous rider of La Bastida, which is precious on account not only of its exceptional quality but of the archaeological context in which it was discovered (late fifth or early fourth century). It is of the same size as the earlier equestrian figure but its proportions are very different. The head is directly derived from those small Greek bronzes with plumed helmets (in this case enormously exaggerated). Here again the warrior is restraining his horse with his left hand, but his right hand wields his unsheathed *falcata* (pl. I).

Stone sculpture

Stone sculpture appeared later in Spain than bronze work, which is scarcely surprising. Greater skill is required to express in stone what is easily produced by modelling wax or clay. Greek archaic art evolved in much the same way.

Sculpture: the creative genius of Iberia

Nevertheless from the outset, the siting of finds poses a problem to the archaeologist. While bronze work originated in the Tartessian region, the first examples of large scale sculpture are found in south-eastern Spain, doubtless under the direct influence of archaic Greek art. Here the role of Asiatic statuary is a minor one, in spite of appearances. As in the case of bronze sculpture, we find a preliminary archaic phase, but the indigenous characteristics are far less marked. A. García y Bellido has in fact described it as 'provincial Greek art'. Greek influence undoubtedly came in through the Phocean settlements in the trade posts of the Spanish Levant, which brought native artists into direct contact with Greek art.

A first group of sculptures consists of fantastic animals of obviously Asiatic origin: for instance, griffins, sphinxes and androcephalic bulls, which had been taken over by the Greeks quite early. These animals were supposed to have protective power over both the dead and the living in Asia and in Greece, but this magical role very quickly came to be accompanied, and presently supplanted, by a purely decorative function. It is not known whether this development took place in Iberia too, but at all events the funerary role of these animal figures is demonstrated by their presence in necropolei. The most famous of these statues is undoubtedly the man-headed bull in the Madrid museum. Familiarly known to the Spaniards as the Beast of Balazote (a village near Albacete), it is worked on one side only and probably stood against a wall. Its head, with the large staring eyes, is of 'sub-Daedalic' type and the body is clumsily treated. García y Bellido has put forward the hypothesis of an imitation of Sicilian coins bearing the image of Achelous.

Even less indigenous is the attractive sphinx from Haches-Bogarra (Albacete) in the Albacete museum. The body seems to be unfinished; the face is framed with plaits in Iberian style, yet it has an Ionian charm with its round cheeks, its almond-shaped eyes, its subtle smile and full lips.

The oldest stone sculpture of a human figure found in

*41 Alicante (?). Woman's head carved from
limestone. Sixth century. Height 23 cm.*
(Archaeological Museum, Barcelona)

Spain is certainly the head (fig. 41) – in the Barcelona
museum – from Alicante, possibly from a site close to Akra
Leuké as yet unidentified. García y Bellido thinks it is a
kore imitated from Attic models, whereas H. Schubart considers it rather an indigenous work akin to the Dama de
Elche. The influence of the art of the Greek islands, of mid-
sixth-century Ionian art, is more probable than that of Attic
art. The exaggeratedly Oriental character of the eye, the
waves of the hair, the high *stephané* (crown) with palms, all
suggest a native artist, as does the squareness of the chin.

Sculpture: the creative genius of Iberia

We must also ascribe to the archaic period, from the mid-sixth to the mid-fifth centuries, a series – unfortunately somewhat fragmentary – of '*damas* seated in majesty', votive offerings or funerary statues (perhaps also deities). The finest examples are those from Verdolay (Murcia) and El Llano de la Consolación (Albacete). The 'hand holding a poppy' from Elche belonged to a statue of this type, probably somewhat later. The copious draperies and the necklace are like those of the Dama de Elche.

The middle period of Iberian sculpture

Towards the end of the fifth century Iberian sculpture presumably had at its disposal a certain number of established forms, created from foreign models more or less transformed. These figures – men in short tunics, ladies in robes, seated ladies, sleeping animals – had sometimes evolved within the archaic tradition, as we have noticed in the case of the equestrian figures. But the characteristics of archaism – whether that of the original model, of the primitive indigenous style or of a mixture of the two – were still prevalent everywhere.

By the end of the fifth or the beginning of the fourth century – it is impossible to fix the date more exactly – we see a new orientation developing in Iberian sculpture, leading to what in my view is its middle period, and which has been termed by M. Almagro its expressive and by E. Cuadrado its Iberian Classical period. These three terms are perfectly self-explanatory although I should prefer to avoid the word Classical. There was never anything approaching Classicism in Iberian art. Sculpture especially retained right to the end, almost into Roman times, archaic or rather archaistic features. Yet between the real archaism of the sixth and fifth centuries and the 'preserved' archaism of the middle and Ibero-Roman periods there is so great a difference that it seems difficult, except in the case of certain rather clumsy sculptures, not to distinguish between them.

What are the characteristics of this 'preserved' archaism? Consider for instance the frontal treatment of figures. Almost all archaic sculptures of the sixth and fifth centuries are presented frontally; the figures are somewhat stiff, symmetrical and all on one plane. This characteristic subsists to the end, at any rate in certain works. In fact it becomes even more marked. In the archaic period for instance the sculptor would merely truncate the back of the head. At a later date, the whole of the back was often sacrificed for the sake of a frontal effect. The same is true of the schematic or geometrical treatment of certain elements: the features of a face, the folds of a garment. This schematism was later intensified. The proportions or the exaggeration of certain details, to which we have already referred, became even more marked. Archaic characteristics were more or less diluted in the process of these transformations.

Why did this occur? The middle period witnessed a considerable development in artistic production, as is indicated by the stone and bronze sculpture that has come down to us. Archaic forms were often repeated, losing certain characteristics in the course of time and becoming simpler and more schematic. Fresh forms appeared, but these from the start displayed the schematic characteristics of the new sculpture which was generally more indigenous than that which had preceded it.

Production was concentrated in sanctuaries which had already been frequented in the archaic period: Despeñaperros, Castellar de Santisteban, Llano de la Consolación, Cerro de los Santos, Verdolay, but also in other sites such as El Cigarralejo and Elche. As we gather from this list, most of the great centres were situated in Upper Andalusia and in the south-east. Lower Andalusia indeed seems to have undergone a temporary decline in creativity, while in Catalonia, Lower Aragon and the region of Valencia the production of sculpture was still meagre.

It must be stressed that these conclusions are based on the

present state of archaeological discoveries, and might perhaps be invalidated by further excavation. In the meantime this uneven distribution remains unexplained. If during the archaic period the centres of production were naturally distributed along the roads to the interior and the coastal zone, this was no longer the case in the fourth and third centuries, when Iberian civilisation had spread inland and even over the Pyrenees, as the discoveries of pottery and metal objects would seem to prove.

The Elche sculpture

It was most likely during the second half of the fifth century that Elche became a highly important artistic centre, particularly notable for its large-scale sculpture. We have mentioned the 'Lady with the Poppies', probably the last of an archaic series of *damas* seated in majesty. A work which may be contemporary, and consequently one of the earliest of this school, is the famous Dama de Elche, the most celebrated of all ancient Spanish sculptures (pl. V) until the very recent (1971) discovery of the splendid Dama de Baza (Granada) (pl. VII).

There is something inexplicable and almost magical about the fame of the Dama de Elche. She is as well-known as the Venus de Milo, the Victory of Samothrace or the Mona Lisa. In Spain the first thing a child learns, once he can read and write, is the existence of the Dama de Elche. The Mona Lisa has been described as a psycho-social phenomenon and a study along these lines might well be made in connection with the bust in the Madrid museum.

Its discovery on 4 August 1897 caused a sensation in the hamlet of La Alcudia, near Elche, where a workman had dug it up on the *finca* (the estate) of Dr Campello. It was exhibited on a stool on the balcony of the house and the village people, filing past it in silence, promptly christened it '*La Reina Mora*'. The news of the find spread to Madrid, London and Berlin. Pierre Paris, who happened to be passing through

Elche, decided to acquire this 'dazzling masterpiece', as he wrote later in his *Promenades archéologiques* (1910). A fortnight after his discovery, he succeeded in buying the bust for the Louvre for the sum of 4,000 francs (the equivalent of 20,000 in 1974). The Dama de Elche was to return to Spain in 1941; she was welcomed as a great lady and exhibited in the Prado museum.

We cannot mention here the extraordinary number of books, articles and commentaries inspired by the Dama de Elche ever since the first account in the *Monuments Piot* in 1898. Scientific arguments about the bust are still going on. They are chiefly concerned with the influences that the work reveals, its connection with indigenous art and its date, but the three problems are obviously interlinked. The sources of this outstanding piece of sculpture are clear enough, but surprising. It is in fact one of the few Iberian sculptures in which we can recognise an imitation of Classical Greek art.

Some time ago R. Carpenter suggested a comparison between the Dama's face and that of the Chatsworth Apollo, that great Attic bronze found in Cyprus and now in the British Museum. The likeness is so evident that one wonders whether the Iberian sculptor had not a statue of this period before his eyes while working at his bust. Furthermore, in spite of its 'Oriental' appearance, this bust undeniably displays indigenous characteristics, while its workmanship is of the highest quality.

Apart from the local limestone from which it was carved, and its polychromy, which was usual at that period, there are two characteristic features: the dress and the jewellery. The Dama's mitre is akin to those shown in the bronzes of Despeñaperros, contemporary or somewhat earlier. Possibly of Oriental origin, it had been the customary headgear of high-born Iberian ladies for a long time when the Elche bust was made. The treatment of the veil or mantle covering the shoulders, with its geometrical folds, is common in the sculpture of the south-east. Under this mantle we can see another, draped over the left shoulder, and finally a tunic whose neckline can be made out underneath the necklaces. These three garments are commonly depicted on statuettes of the archaic and middle periods and are frequently seen on stone sculptures. As for the jewellery, large *bullae* like those on the lower necklace have been discovered in Tartessian treasures, such as that of Aliseda. The small amphora-pendants and the large wheels on either side of the head are more puzzling. However, discs placed in similar fashion have been found on three or four statues in the Cerro de los Santos.

Under these circumstances, what date should be assigned

*42 La Alcudia (Elche, Alicante). Limestone
bust of warrior. Fourth century. (Museum
of La Alcudia)*

to the Dama de Elche? In my opinion R. Carpenter's comparison with the Chatsworth Apollo is decisive, and there is no reason to speak of 'preserved archaism' in this connection. However, the relatively schematic treatment of the dress reflects the evolution that had taken place since the archaic period. The bust must therefore be assumed to belong to the threshold of the middle period, in the second half of the fifth century. Many authors have argued that this theory cannot be maintained since busts did not appear in sculpture until a much later date. But we are not dealing with Greece. The final problem posed by the Dama de Elche is that of her function. The figure has been variously interpreted as an image to be worshipped, a votive offering, the portrait of a princess. Unquestionably it was also primarily a funerary statue, as were the various ladies seated in majesty, and all of them may have represented deities.

The quality of '*La Reina Mora*' puts all the other Elche statues far into the shade. Even so, these are of great interest, and it is not impossible that the excavation being made on the site by the present owner of La Alcudia, A. Ramos Folques, may some day produce important discoveries.

Of a much later date are the two pieces which, despite the difference of their subject, are related to the Elche bust by their lively and expressive character. A bust of a warrior (fig. 42) suggests interesting comparisons with other Iberian works. Over a short tunic such as we find on many bronzes, the folds of which are clearly shown above the belt, he wears a double baldric decorated with teeth or acorns, which holds a large breastplate depicting a grinning wolf's head. These are all protective signs, which recur on a piece from the Tivisa treasure (fig. 118). There is also a concave shield in which the sculptor has depicted the handle and its fastenings with meticulous realism and carved the warrior's hand in lifelike fashion; we could ask for no better illustration of the way the Iberians held their shields (fig. 43).

Sculpture: the creative genius of Iberia

El Llano de la Consolación and El Cerro de los Santos

In these two sanctuaries, which are only a few kilometres apart, and particularly in the latter, a considerable collection of sculptures has been discovered. Here again it would appear that the position of the sites at a natural cross-roads, favouring contact with the coastal zone, promoted the development of a whole school of sculpture, this time in stone.

Stylistically the sculptures of these two sites are fairly closely related. But the artistic activity of El Llano de la Consolación must certainly have preceded that of El Cerro de los Santos. Thus a Lady in Majesty (formerly in the

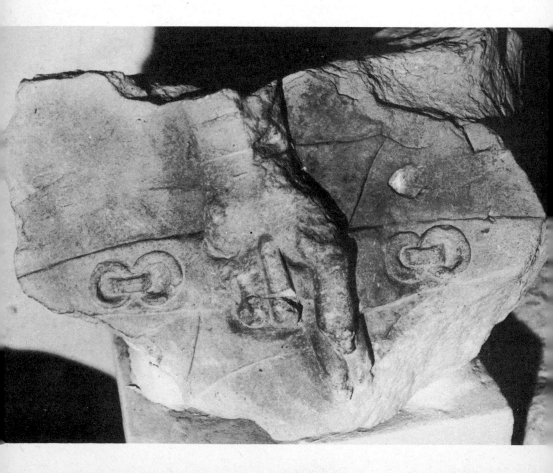

43 Opposite: *La Alcudia (Elche, Alicante). Fragment showing a hand holding a buckler. Fourth or third century.* (Museum of La Alcudia)

44 Below: *Llano de la Consolación (Montealegre, Albacete) Man's head carved from limestone. Fifth century. Height 22 cm.* (Louvre, Paris)

Louvre) was found there, which dates from the late archaic or early middle period, well into the fifth century. This figure clearly shows the impact of Greek influence on indigenous sculpture.

The same is true of the magnificent stone head which the Louvre is fortunate enough to own (fig. 44). Contemporary with the seated figure, this still shows some features of Ionian archaism about the eyes and in the five curious wavy locks around the forehead. But all this is diluted in a characteristically indigenous treatment in broad planes, which conveys with great intensity the inward-looking character of Iberian art.

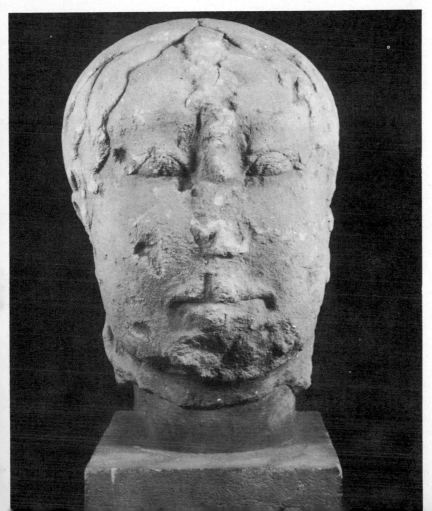

45 *Cerro de los Santos (Montealegre, Albacete). Woman bearing libation vessel carved in limestone. Fourth or third century.* (National Archaeological Museum, Madrid)

46 *Cerro de los Santos(Montealegre, Albacete). Woman bearing libation vessel.* (National Archaeological Museum, Madrid)

A. Fernández de Avilés considered that the sculpture of El Cerro began at the end of the fifth century and went on until the Roman period. It is unquestionable that the art of El Cerro was inspired by that of the neighbouring sanctuary. But it developed considerably during the fourth and third centuries, producing several hundreds – thousands, perhaps if we take into account the number that have disappeared – of votive offerings of all sorts and sizes, almost all of which are

47 *Cerro de los Santos (Montealegre, Albacete). Woman's head carved in limestone. Fifth or fourth century. Height 17 cm. (Louvre, Paris)*

of stone. Most of these represent richly clad female figures, seated in majesty or standing, holding the libation vessel in both hands (fig. 45). Others are represented only as busts, like the Dama de Elche.

Finally there is a vast series of votive heads, including a number of male heads; incidentally full-length figures of men are rare. The statuary of El Cerro has not yet received the full-scale description it deserves. A comparative study of

Sculpture: the creative genius of Iberia

these sculptures with the fourth-century Dama de Baza would make it possible to establish their chronology.

Among the pieces reproduced here the Gran Dama Oferente (fig. 14) in the Madrid museum is certainly one of the richest and most interesting. One is struck first by its frontal character. The statue was intended to be looked at solely from the front, so that seen in profile the lower part seems to be thrust forward. The dress consists of veils, mantles and skirts superimposed on one another. The ornaments are sumptuous: a plaited wig to which are fixed the diadem and two discs, smaller than those of the Dama de Elche but even more finely worked. The treatment of the face is typically indigenous of the Iberian middle period; the geometrical character of the garment's folds reveals the evolution of form since the time of the majestic archaic figures and the Dama de

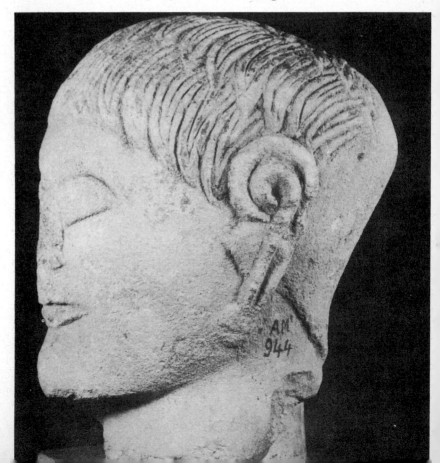

48 *Cerro de los Santos (Montealegre, Albacete). Man's head, carved in limestone. Fourth century. Height 26 cm.* (Louvre, Paris)

49 *Baena (Cordoba). Stone lioness. Fourth or third century. Height 26 cm.* (National Archaeological Museum, Madrid)

Elche. This Gran Dama clearly belongs to the fourth century. Of a later date are the more schematic figures such as the Dama from the Madrid museum (fig. 46), where the sculptor has suggested the folds of the shawl from which the mitre emerges by large inverted chevrons. Later still, more realistic draperies were to reappear under Hellenistic and Roman influence.

The sculpture of heads developed in much the same way; at first showing clear signs of Greek influence (fig. 47), they assumed a wholly Iberian vigour in such male portraits as the one in the Louvre (fig. 48), where the continued archaism of the face is combined with the geometrical treatment of the hair – a remote Ionian heritage – which is not represented

at the back of the head. The ears and the ear-pendants, which
were commonly worn by men in the south-east, are exaggerated and highly stylised in whorls or scrolls.

Zoomorphic sculpture

During the middle period, particularly in the fourth century,
we find an increase in the number of zoomorphic sculptures in
which bulls and lions are preponderant, throughout an area
spreading beyond Iberian borders into Celtic regions (fig. 1).
We have already mentioned the Oriental or Mediterranean
origin of these animals whose function was to protect the
living and the dead. Here again indigenous characteristics
grow more marked in the course of evolution: forms become
more massive, volumes are disconnected and angular, appear-
ing like broad, almost flat, surfaces.

The Lioness of Baena (Cordoba) in the Madrid museum
is typical (fig. 49). Sometimes only the head has been
sculpted, but with remarkable artistry (fig. 50). Most frequently – and this tendency was more conspicuous in the
Roman period – muscles, commissures and hair are indicated
schematically by incisions which form almost geometrical
patterns, as on the Bull of Porcuna (Jaén) in the Jaén
museum (fig. 51), the tip of whose tail resembles a stylised
lotus bud.

This fondness for detail recurs in the head of another bull
in the Jaén museum, where the tuft of hair between the eyes
has been rendered as an outsize rosette (fig. 52). A final,
and perhaps the most recent, example comes from Saguntum.
The eyes and nostrils of this bull are surrounded by great
parallel incisions. The mouth is borrowed from the lion-type.
This kind of mutation is not unusual in Iberian plastic art
(fig. 53).

El Cigarralejo and the Iberian horses

El Cigarralejo (Mula, Murcia) represents a special case
among Iberian sanctuaries. More recently excavated (in

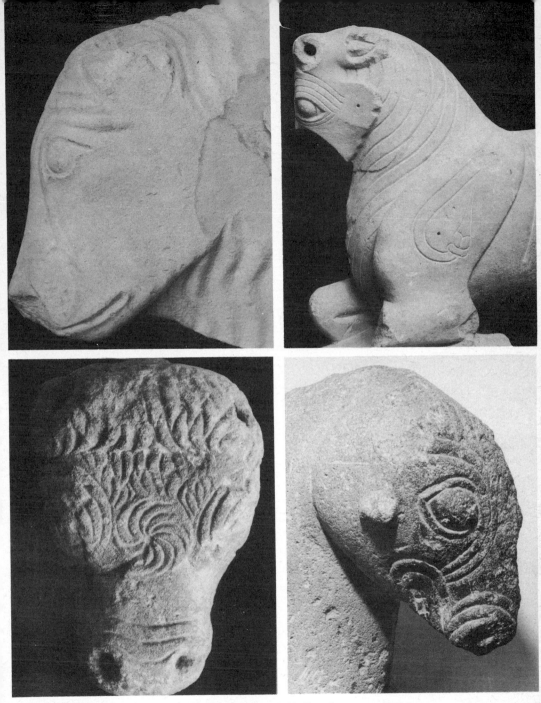

50 Top left: *Arjona (Granada). Detail of a stone bull. Fourth century. Height of head 38 cm.* (Archaeological Museum, Granada)

51 Top right: *Porcuna (Jaén). Stone bull. Fourth or third century. Length 75 cm.* (Archaeological Museum, Jaén)

52 Lower left: *Province of Jaén (?). Bull's head. Third century. Length 27 cm.* (Archaeological Museum, Jaén)

53 Lower right: *Sagunto (Valencia). Detail of bull. Third century.* (Archaeological Museum, Sagunto)

1947) than the others, it enjoyed the advantage of the latest
methods of archaelogical prospecting, thanks to E. Cuadrado
who succeeded in distinguishing three strata. The second,
corresponding to an Iberian sanctuary of the fourth and third
centuries, yielded a number of stone votive offerings consisting
of some twenty human figures and a hundred representing
horses, almost all of great interest. The human figures are
warriors in cloaks or standing *damas*, and are akin stylistically
both to those of the Andalusian sanctuaries of the middle
period (see below) and to those of El Cerro de los Santos;
this can be accounted for by the position of Cigarralejo on
the road running along the upper Segura, leading from the
south-east to Upper Andalusia. But these votive offerings
have an undeniable individuality.

The same is true of the horses. A 'Master of Cigarralejo' has
been postulated as creator of the finest of these impressive
fourth-century works.

Their realism distinguishes them totally from all the
zoomorphic figures we have seen hitherto. These are not
derivative works based on indigenous archaic prototypes,
but original figures inspired by Classical models: see for
instance the magnificent harnessed horse (fig. 54). So sensitive is the treatment of form and the interconnection of
volumes that, in spite of the archaistic appearance of the head
and neck, this work seems to stand on the frontier of Classicism. In the precise treatment of detail in the bridle, martin-
gale and saddle-blanket we recognise the hand of the Iberian
artist, who incidentally gives us by this means valuable
information about the harness in antiquity.

The other horses of El Cigarralejo are not of the same
quality. Therefore we must assume that the form deteriorated
by dint of repetition. We still need to find out to what god
these offerings were dedicated. Was there some tutelary
deity for horses in Iberia or was this sanctuary specially
frequented by horsemen or mounted warriors? We have no
answer to these questions. There is nothing surprising,

54 El Cigarralejo (Mula, Murcia).
Sandstone horse in harness. Fourth century.
Length 1·6 metres

however, about the great number of these horses. Equestrian figures seem to have had either a protective or a funerary function in Iberia, or perhaps both at once, as countless examples suggest. But there are few figures of men on horseback at El Cigarralejo.

The deity of this sanctuary was probably akin to that 'master of animals' who appears on a relief from Mogón (Jaén) in the Jaén museum. (fig. 22). Here the god is represented as a man dressed in a short belted tunic. He is taming two rearing horses, which are stylistically related to the fourth-century figures of El Cigarralejo. On the *stele* from Villaricos

Sculpture: the creative genius of Iberia

(Almeria) (fig. 23), which is of a later date, the seated figure has two faces, but is probably the same deity.

Bronze votive offerings

After the archaic period, which had witnessed the creation of finely wrought prototypes, Iberian bronze sculpture evolved in two directions. First we have the advent of what has been described as 'mass produced' art. The main archaic forms persist, but they are simplified by the omission of certain details and the schematisation of the remaining elements, with a general tendency towards 'preserved archaism'. The enormous increase in output even led to the production of minute figurines like sticks or pins, some only 2 to 3 centimetres in height.

This mass production, however, did not preclude the creation of new types of equestrian figures, men in cloaks and ladies in tall mitres. There are also some very fine examples of nude figurines, both male and female.

In this twofold evolution, but particularly in the new forms created, the indigenous character becomes more defined. This is the 'Golden Age' of Iberianism. A bronze from Despeñaperros, now in the Madrid museum (fig. 6), illustrates both aspects of the middle period. In this tiny equestrian group (52 centimetres in height) the rider still has an archaic appearance. His diadem and short embroidered tunic suggest a personage of high rank.

The horse on the other hand illustrates the new tendency. Another horseman from the Museo Valencia de Don Juan in Madrid (fig. 4) recalls the figure from La Bastida (pl. I). But one can recognise the evolution that has taken place, the more so as this piece probably belongs to the end of the middle period, being one of its last masterpieces. Moreover, a tendency towards realism is displayed at this period in the small bronze animal-figures of the south-eastern region, such as the horses of El Cigarralejo or the delightful little fourth-century ox from La Bastida (fig. 55). The men in short

55 La Bastida de les Alcuses (Mogente, Valencia). Bronze figurine of an ox. Fourth century. Length 4·1 cm.

tunics, who are presumably unarmed warriors, are often shown in unfamiliar forms.

At Despeñaperros and later at Castellar there are figures of worshippers with outstretched arms; towards the end of the period these take on a touching quality, as in the figure in the Barcelona museum, who is wearing a leather cap or possibly a wig with plaits attached (pl. IV). A new type of male figure is represented by the warrior in a long double cloak fastened on the right shoulder, offering up his weapons to his god (fig. 9).

The statuettes of women are somewhat disappointing. They naturally include examples derived from archaic forms, such as the votaress in a mitre and long enveloping robe in the Municipal museum at Valencia (fig. 56), or the more massive statuette in the Madrid museum wrapped in a flounced veil, holding up her enormous right hand in

56 Province of Jaén (?). Bronze statuette of votaress with mitre. Fifth or fourth century. (Municipal Museum, Valencia)

57 Despeñaperros (Santa Elena, Jaén). Bronze statuette of votaress. Fourth century. Height 11.2 cm. (National Archaeological Museum, Madrid)

salutation to the god – an Oriental concept (fig. 57). However, these are merely the last representatives of a prolific line.

A few quite unfamiliar types are included among the female figures. There are ladies in tall mitres and veils with long points that look somewhat like spearheads seen from behind; an example of this category is the votaress in the Museo Valencia de Don Juan (fig. 58), with outstretched hands and knees slightly bent, like the men with plaited hair already mentioned. Other statuettes seem freely inspired by stone sculpture, acquiring thereby a wealth of detail but losing something of the grace and lightness which were the property of archaic sculpture.

The famous 'priestess with necklaces' from Castellar de

I La Bastida de los Alcuses (Mogente, Valencia). Bronze warrior on horseback. Fifth or fourth century. Height 7·1 cm. (Museum of Prehistory, Valencia)

Cerro de San Miguel (Liria, Valencia). Detail from the 'warriors vase' (cf. fig.95)

Ia   Castellar de Santisteban (Jaén). Bronze statuette of nude votary. Middle period.
Height 11 cm. (Archaeological Museum, Barcelona)
Ib   Despeñaperros (?) Bronze statuette of woman bearing offerings. Sixth century. Height
9 cm. (Municipal Museum, Vich (Gerona))
Ic   Castellar de Santisteban (Jaén). Late bronze statuette of naked warrior armed with
falcata and caetra. Height 6·6 cm. (Archaeological Museum, Barcelona)
Id   Castellar de Santisteban (Jaén). 'Priestess with necklaces'. Bronze statuette of votaress.
Fourth century. Height 7·5 cm. (Archaeological Museum, Barcelona)

IV Castellar de Santisteban
(Jaén). *Bronze statuette of votary.*
Fourth century. Height 10·5 *cm.*
(Archaeological Museum,
Barcelona)

La Alcudia (Elche, Alicante). The 'Dama de Elche'
carved from polychrome limestone. Second half of fifth century.
(National Archaeological Museum, Madrid)

VII   Baza (Granada). The 'Dama de Baza' ▶
carved from polychrome limestone. Fourth
century. (National Archaeological Museum,
Madrid)

VIa   Cerro de San Miguel (Liria, Valencia).
Cylindrical vase. Third century. Height 25 cm.
(Museum of Prehistory, Valencia)
VIb   El Cabecico del Tesoro (Verdolay,
Murcia). Reverse side of kalathos shown in
fig. 81
VIc   El Cabecico del Tesoro (Verdolay,
Murcia). Carnassiers (wild beasts) vase. Third
or second century. Height 30 cm. (Museum of
Prehistory, Valencia)

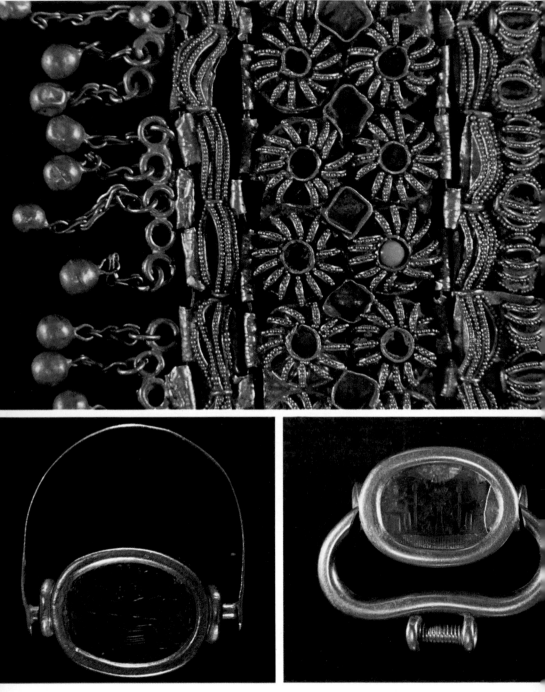

VIIIb   Aliseda (Cáceres). Seal-ring worked in gold and agate. Seventh century. External diameter 2 cm. (National Archaeological Museum, Madrid)

VIIIc   Aliseda (Cáceres). Seal made from gold and amethyst. Seventh century. External diameter 4·3 cm. (National Archaeological Museum, Madrid)

58 Despeñaperros (?). Bronze statuette of votaress. Fourth or third century. Height 10·2 cm. (Valencia de Don Juan Museum, Madrid)

59 Despeñaperros (?). Bronze statuettes, representing schematic female figures. Middle period. (Municipal Museum, Valencia)

145

Santisteban, now in the Barcelona museum, is a miniature Dama de Elche, with her mitre, her 'wheels' and her two neck-laces (pl. IIId). In the museum at Albacete we can see another Dama (found 1 kilometre from the sanctuary of El Cerro de los Santos) which is a kind of simplified copy of the large stone statues from the same sanctuary.

It is amusing to trace the repetition of form in the schematic figures which some writers have described as mass-produced. We find two ladies in pointed mitres, one with a light, the other with a dark patina, both undoubtedly fashioned at a few days' or even perhaps at a few hours' interval by the same craftsman, out of a square metal rod, hammered and filed and then incised with a graver to indicate the dress and arms (fig. 59). These were the votive offerings of the poor, even though they represent a rich lady in a mitre.

Finally we must mention the nudes, so strangely akin to modern tastes and as distant as can be from any principles of Classicism. They reveal the very heart of Iberian sensibility, while remaining close to the most elementary symbolism. The warrior from Despeñaperros offers up his weapons (fig. 60). The statuette consists of this single gesture. The feminine equivalent exists; the craftsman has merely changed the sexual organs and replaced the weapons with fruit. The same comment can be made about the nude male figure from Castellar in the Barcelona museum. His body is a mere cylinder with an inordinately large penis to ensure divine protection (pl. IIIa). Compare with this figure that of the naked woman (fig. 61), reduced to the simple and touching expression of a prayer.

The late period of Iberian sculpture

During the second half of the third century Iberian plastic art took a new turn. This may perhaps have been the result of political upheavals due to the Barcid conquest, which met with some hostility outside the Tartessian region. It might have been expected that these events would destroy artistic activity in Iberia. Yet such was the creative vigour of the Iberians that they now found fresh inspiration in Hellenistic Mediterranean art and were later to endeavour to assimilate that of Rome.

Certain centres such as El Cigarralejo disappeared during the second Punic war at the end of the third century, but others survived in Despeñaperros, Castellar de Santisteban, El Cerro de los Santos, to mention only a few. During the third century a new sanctuary, La Serreta near Alcoy, began producing a large number of terracotta figures. And not unexpectedly there was a revival of stone sculpture in Lower Andalusia, in the region of Seville and more particularly in Osuna.

60 Despeñaperros (Santa Elena, Jaén). Bronze statuette of naked warrior. Fourth or third century. Height 11·5 cm. (National Archaeological Museum, Madrid)

61 Nude votaress. Middle period. (Municipal Museum, Valencia)

Late bronzes

Contact with Hellenistic art, probably through the intermediary of ceramics and minor *objets d'art*, introduced into Iberian bronze sculpture the expression of movement and a certain pathos, a tendency which was already evident in the preceding period. The statuettes of warriors and male nudes are representative of this new trend. A small warrior from Castellar is shown approaching the god, with his hands out-outstretched, not touching his *falcata* or the round buckler slung on his back (pl. IIIc). Another warrior from Despeñaperros brandishes his spear obliquely, thus departing from the almost obligatory symmetry of these figurines (fig. 62).

Probably the enormous penis has its usual protective function, as in the bronze (fig. 63), possibly of the Roman period, which is now in the Madrid museum. We also note at this period bronzes representing the emaciated figures of the sick in attitudes of supplication (fig. 64), or small, massive statuettes of singular intensity (fig. 65).

Special consideration must be given to the bronze sculpture of the south-east, which developed around the sanctuary of La Luz, near the city of Verdolay. Here we find strange figurines such as that of the veiled lady in a short skirt and boots with broad cuffs (fig. 16). But it was under the influence of Roman art that La Luz produced its finest pieces: a vase-bearer in the Barcelona museum, with an expression of great

62 Despeñaperros (Santa Elena, Jaén). Late bronze statuette of naked warrior holding spear. Height 7·8 cm. (National Archaeological Museum, Madrid)

63 Monteagudo (Murcia) (?). Bronze warrior in a short tunic. Roman period. Height 12 cm. (National Archaeological Museum, Madrid)

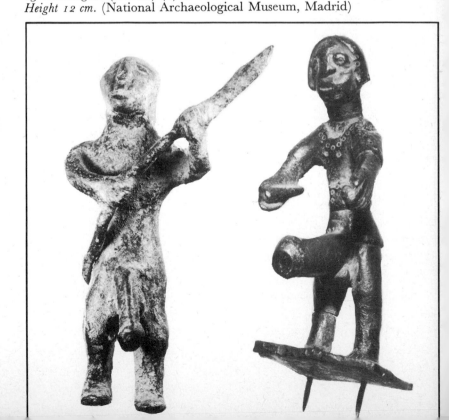

concentration, or the tall equestrian figure, upright and stiff, presumably from the first century A.D. (fig. 66). One wonders, finally, whether to class as Iberian or Roman the man in a mantle from the Madrid museum (fig. 8), decorously covering himself with a fold of his garment, like so many figures from El Cerro de los Santos. The drapery and the border of the cloak are borrowed from some *togatus*, while the expression displays a manly serenity that is typically Roman.

Terracotta figures

Modelling or moulding in clay does not seem to have been held in as high esteem by the Iberians as it was by the Greeks and Carthaginians, until the third century B.C.

64 Despeñaperros (Santa Elena, Jaén). Late bronze statuette of a sick man. Height 11 cm. (National Archaeological Museum, Madrid)

65 Castellar de Santisteban (Jaén). Bronze statuette of a female figure. Roman period. Height 6·9 cm. (Archaeological Museum, Barcelona)

66 *La Luz* (*Verdolay,
Murcia*). *Mounted
warrior in bronze. First
century* A.D. *Height
12·5 cm.* (Archaeo-
logical Museum,
Barcelona)

67 La Serreta (Alcoy, Alicante). Terracotta head. Third or second century. Height 8 cm. (Archaeological Museum, Alcoy)

68 El Tossal de los Tenalles (Sidamunt, Lérida). Lid from a vase. Third century. Diameter 8 cm. (Archaeological Museum, Barcelona)

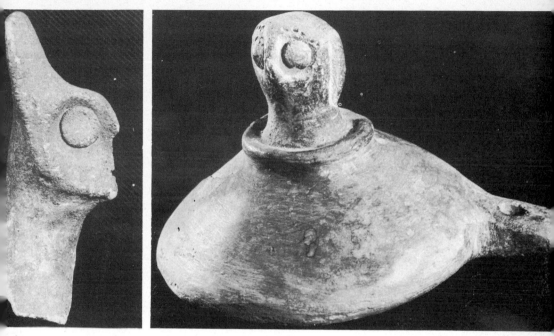

Except in the Balearic Islands, where production came under Phoenician and Carthaginian influence, we find only a few sporadic examples of terracotta figures. Their number cannot compare with the thousands of bronze votive offerings of which we have spoken. From the third century onwards a few clay figurines are found in many places, but the industry was centred chiefly at La Serreta near Alcoy, where thousands of pieces must have been produced, right up to the late Roman empire.

The votive figures of Alcoy can be divided into two groups, probably contemporaneous. The first comprises rudimentary figurines modelled between finger and thumb, with the eyes stuck on (fig. 67), or merely indicated by incised lines of varying breadth. This was the usual technique in Iberia, as we see from a vase-lid from Tossal de Los Tenalles (fig. 68). This extremely naïve art is not devoid of aesthetic interest and indeed attains a rare quality in the scene that depicts the worship of the Mother Goddess (fig. 19).

The pieces in the second category are less interesting, being imitations of Hellenistic or Roman votive offerings in terracotta (fig. 69). Yet both kinds show powerful indigenous characteristics in their proportions and of course in the rendering of head-dress or hair style, dress and jewellery, with which Iberian artists were always particularly concerned.

Finally a tiny bust of the early second century, discovered in the neighbourhood of Alicante, shows a harmonious blending of the last traces of archaism in a style borrowed from Hellenistic or Roman art (fig. 70).

69 La Serreta (Alcoy, Alicante). Fragment of terracotta statuette, representing a female figure. Roman period. Height of fragment 6·5 cm. (Archaeological Museum, Alcoy)

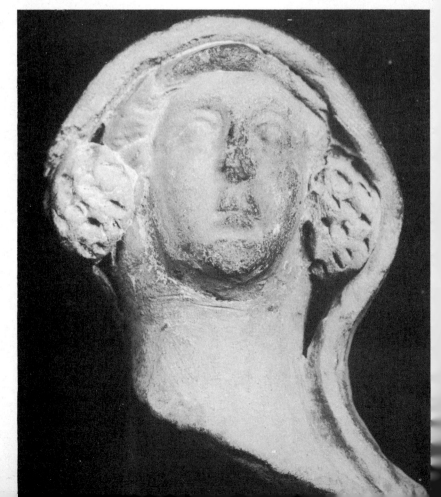

The high reliefs of Osuna

The Iberian fortress of Osuna was explored at the beginning of the present century by two French archaeologists, Pierre Paris and A. Engel. At that time excavations were not conducted in a strictly methodical fashion and their impressive collection of finds was made without any reference to archaeological context. None the less, a stylistic study of these objects suggests that they range from the third century B.C. to the time of the Roman Empire.

70 El Tossal de Manises (Alicante). Man's head in terracotta. Second century. Height 13.5 cm. (Provincial Archaeological Museum, Alicante)

The sculpture of Osuna is interesting because of its great diversity, and we may assume that many sculptors from various parts of Iberia came to work there. For instance we can clearly trace the characteristics of Celtic art in the fragment (fig. 71), now in the Madrid museum, of a group showing a man laid low by a fantastic animal. The Osuna centre was undoubtedly more open than those of El Cerro de los Santos or El Cigarralejo, the style of which is more homogeneous and more traditional.

The reliefs of Osuna, whether intended for the decoration of some religious edifice or merely as votive offerings, represent ladies in procession, warriors and horsemen. They may be divided into two groups according to their workmanship: the first is more characteristically indigenous and is probably the older. It is represented by the charging warrior in the Madrid museum, half hidden by his long shield (the *scutum*) and holding his bare *falcata* in his right hand. With his great

71 Osuna (Seville). Fragment of a limestone high relief depicting a man attacked by a monstrous animal. Third or second century. Height 40 cm. (Archaeological Museum, Madrid)

72 Osuna (Seville). Attacking warriors in limestone relief. Third or second century. Height 74 cm. (Louvre, Paris)

crested helmet on his head, he cuts a dashing figure. But the warrior in the Louvre, preparing to strike a mighty blow with his sword, shows finer workmanship and a better-proportioned silhouette (fig. 72).

More primitive still is the enigmatic relief of 'the kiss' (fig. 73). All these examples of the Tartessian tradition have been influenced not only by Celtic art from the interior of Spain but also by Hellenistic art, from which the sculptors learned to elongate their forms and above all to express movement. The other group, which is unmistakably Ibero-Roman, includes a remarkable figure of a man blowing a horn, an acrobat, and a procession of warriors.

73 Osuna (Seville). 'The kiss' carved in sandstone relief. Third or second century. Length 22 cm. (National Archaeological Museum, Madrid)

CHAPTER 7
Iberian painted
pottery

Even today the rich field of Iberian painted pottery has by no means been fully explored. In the first place it is, like sculpture, a precious source of information about the religion, society and daily life of the ancient Iberians, of which archaeologists and historians have made much use.

The art historian might find abundant material in the study of the shapes of Iberian vases and the draughtsmanship, composition and iconography of their painted decoration, problems which have not been adequately tackled hitherto. Furthermore, in spite of the many valuable studies which have been published in recent years, Iberian pottery has not proved as helpful to the archaeologist as, for instance, Greek or Gallo-Roman potsherds are today. The problem of chronology, although it has made undeniable progress, has not in fact been definitely solved.

It is not our purpose here to enter into the details of this question of dating, with which archaeologists have been concerned since the beginning of the present century. One paramount difficulty arises from the fact that Iberian pottery was primarily produced for local use, with a large number of workshops satisfying relatively limited requirements. None the less, it was diffused beyond the frontiers of Spain, since specimens have been found on the Mediterranean coasts of France and Italy. But these scattered finds bear no comparison with the thousands of Greek and Gallo-Roman potsherds, products of an organised export industry, which though dug up far from their place of origin can be reliably dated. As a result the restricted diffusion of Iberian pottery makes it difficult to date.

This, however, is not the sole reason. Local workshops, whose customers were probably not hard to please, produced vases of uneven quality. It is thus difficult to ascribe to them any specific kind of paste, firing process or slip, as can be done accurately for ceramics intended for export. Undoubtedly there are local characteristics, but they are too general.

For this reason, in the early years of the present century, grave errors of dating were made. Pierre Paris, noticing stylistic resemblances with Mycenean pottery, unhesitatingly dated the fine fragments from Elche or Meca as belonging to the thirteenth century B.C., some thousand years too early!

We now know that Iberian pottery only came into existence much later, probably in the sixth century B.C. To begin with, it borrowed forms and techniques from the painted vases of the Mediterranean countries, from Phoenician, Cypriot, Ionian and Attic ware and in some cases from local vases of the first Iron Age. But before long the inventive genius of Spanish potters led them to adapt and alter these forms and decoration to suit their native needs. Thus they created works of incomparable originality, which in their turn were to be supplanted by the sigillated pottery popular throughout Gaul and Spain in the first century B.C.

Shapes

Iberian potters shaped their vases on a wheel. Complete masters of this technique, which was of Mediterranean origin, they succeeded in making large vessels with fine linings, of a sort hitherto unknown. But the pastes varied widely in different regions and workshops and even at different periods in the same workshop; the clays also differed in their degree of refinement and their granular quality.

Generally the vase, after shaping, was covered with a light engobe on which, when it was dry, the decoration was painted with diluted metallic oxides or red earth. Firing was done in great kilns, of which a few specimens have been found, especially in Catalonia. There is one at Fontscaldes (Tarragona) with an underground fireplace, the roof of which was held up by great arches. The smoke came through side flues to the firing chamber, which was built vertically, then presumably passed along other flues to avoid contact with the articles to be fired.

Iberian pottery could perfectly well have been fired in such kilns, but in fact it was probably never subjected to very high temperatures, which would have given it greater toughness. Many of the potsherds discovered during excavation show a break where the centre of the earthenware has remained grey while the two outer layers are light yellow or orange. Grey or grey-green earthenware of fine quality has also been unearthed with the design painted on directly in red.

The shapes are extremely varied, with borrowings from many sources and a great many inventions. They are often described by the names of Greek vases, but this is a mistake, for the Iberians often took ideas from a number of sources to create a single form. Thus one might be tempted to give the name *pithos* to those great jars from Elche or elsewhere which are well painted, having full curves and a narrow foot and are imitated from Greek models.

But other, smaller ones owed something to Punic amphorae, which were copied moreover in the workshops that supplied the necropolis of Galera. An almost identical shape, with the bulge slightly lower down, served as funerary urn in the necropolis of Oliva and again in that of Galera, with a lid fitted to the body in a zigzag pattern. This curious detail recurs in many urns of the same necropolis (fig. 74). More uncommon is the tall cylindrical shape of a vase with a lid from Liria (pl. VIa).

A second group comprises many vases of *kalathos* shape which Spanish archaeologists used to call 'top hats' (*sombreros de copa*) (pl. VIa – VIb). Broad-brimmed and almost cylindrical, these must frequently have been used as urns, to judge by the number of finds; Iberians were particularly fond of this indigenous shape which in some cases included a lid. Some huge specimens, which must have served as jars, have come to light.

Spanish potters, like those of Greece, made *kraters*, sometimes servile copies (fig. 75) or freely created, such as the wide-mouthed, handleless vessels which remotely recall the *kraters* of the Greek archaic period (fig. 89).

The most usual forms of pottery included shallow cylindrical receptacles (fig. 85), large and small bowls with or without feet, a wide variety of plates and dishes with broad raised rims, sometimes with a central knob, which were used

75 Galera (Granada). Krater *with small columns. Fourth*
century. (National Archaeological Museum, Madrid)

for domestic or sacrificial purposes and which distantly echo
Oriental pottery.

Pouring vessels included *oenochoai* (jugs) with low swelling
curves and without feet (fig. 82), double-handled vases and
also tall bell-mouthed pots, of which there were many
examples in the south (fig. 76).

This brief list is obviously incomplete, for potters varied
their forms endlessly by creating intermediary types. It is
occasionally possible to find on a particular site a continuous
evolution of shapes through successive periods, but such a
pattern of development is unfortunately seldom valid outside
that site.

Iberian painted pottery

Geometrical designs in ceramics

The commonest form of ceramic, which is found throughout the Iberian region – so much so that it practically defines the limits of Iberia for the archaeologist – is that decorated with geometrical designs consisting of bands of varying width, concentric circles or semi-circles, zigzags, waves, meanders and so forth, painted in colours ranging from violet-red to dark brown on a light background. The decoration is independent of the shapes, which, as we have seen, vary widely. Recent excavations have disclosed the diverse origins of this pottery.

On 30 September 1958, while work was going on at the shooting-traps of Seville, a magnificent sixth-century hoard came to light at a place called El Carambolo. J. de Mata Carriazo decided to explore the surroundings to make an accurate study of its stratification. Advised by J. Maluquer, he made a discovery which apparently was unconnected with the treasure: the foundations of a hut laid on top of several strata, the earliest of which belonged to the ninth and eighth centuries.

This contained, among other things, sherds of pottery, decorated with concentric bands and rings, and other fragments, in particular those of a hollow jar painted with hatched lines, squares and triangles. Both types were presumably imitated from the Cypriot amphorae which were in circulation throughout the Mediterranean basin, but the second (which its discoverer called Tartessian) is undoubtedly our oldest specimen of geometrically decorated Iberian ware.

H. Schubart has recently published a brief synthesis of these discoveries and of the excavations of the German Institute at Torre del Mar which have made it possible to ascribe a seventh-century date to the first Iberian imitations of Phoenician ceramics with polychromatic bands found in Andalusia and in the Spanish Levant (fig. 77).

Somewhat later, at the beginning of the sixth century,

76 *Galera (Granada). Wide-mouthed vase.*
(National Archaeological Museum,
Madrid)

77 *Galera (Granada). Vase decorated with
bands.* (National Archeological Museum
Madrid)

163

another sort of banded pottery, Ionian this time, was being
copied from the Levant to Catalonia. As far as we can judge
in the present state of archaeological discoveries, these were
the three sources of Iberian geometrical pottery. But here
again native craftsmen considerably enlarged their repertory
and the combinations of geometrical figures within this
style of decoration which persists right up to the Roman
conquest.

We should place in a separate category the red glazed
pottery of Phoenician origin, which was widespread throughout the Peninsula in the fourth century and which probably
had some influence on certain indigenous forms.

There was also a highly original type of plain grey pottery
of fine workmanship, which the Iberians copied at a relatively
late date from Massaliote and then from Campanian models.

But the vases depicting figures naturally deserve our closest attention.

From abstraction to stylisation

Until at least the second century the Iberians stubbornly went on making this geometrical pottery and sometimes achieved felicitous effects with the abstract motifs distributed thickly or thinly over the surface of the vases. Obviously this decoration evolved during the course of five centuries. It is denser and perhaps more harmoniously laid out in south-eastern and Andalusian pottery; elsewhere it remained fairly simple. Within a single site one finds important variations, such as those observed by C. Fernández Chicarro and A. Blanco at Castellones de Ceal (Jaén). These are of interest chiefly to specialists, for the general appearance shows little change – a characteristic in keeping with the customary persistence of techniques and themes in Iberia. We shall see later that wall paintings also reveal the same tendency towards abstract decoration.

Things changed in eastern and south-eastern Spain at the beginning of the third century, with the almost simultaneous emergence of a new kind of decoration in several centres. Schools of painting sprang up which were to persist long after the arrival of the Romans in Spain.

Just as geometrical decoration had appeared under the influence of foreign ceramics, so figure painting took its inspiration from Attic red-figure vases and above all from the Graeco-Italian pottery of the fourth century, often known as Italiote. These were widely diffused throughout Iberia at that time, particularly in south-eastern and Catalonian sites. They are also found, though more sparsely, in Lower and Upper Andalusia, where superb *kraters* have been discovered in the necropolis of Galera.

We may wonder if traditionalism alone explains the reluctance of Iberian potters to adorn the surface of their vases with the plant motifs and scenes of action which were so

widely used by Greek painters from the eighth century onwards. Why does Greek representational painting exert no
influence until the third century? It is not easy to answer
this question, which has already puzzled many archaeologists,
some of whom have indeed sought to solve it against all the
evidence, by attributing a fifth-century date to the appearance of figured decoration in Iberia. In the first place we
must observe that Greek pottery scarcely reached the interior
of Spain before the middle of the fifth century and that it
was not widely used by the Spaniards until the fourth century.
But though the increased importation of Greek ceramics
played some part, it cannot wholly explain the change.

Italiote ceramic art at the beginning of the fourth century
shows a distinct divergence from Attic red-figure pottery.
The Greek painters of southern Italy, Lucania and particularly Apulia, organised the perspective of their scenes, filled
their spaces more completely, and introduced decorative
elements such as palmettes and rosettes within the scenes
themselves. It was this new mode of painting that aroused in
Iberian artists that interest in representation, and that
concern with filling the whole available surface, which we
shall note in their various schools. But they took more than a
lesson in composition from this Italiote pottery; they appreciated its swirling movement of draperies and bodies and its
flexible organisation of lines, which they were to render in
their own fashion.

Once again, as we noticed in the case of sculpture, the
Iberians, who were not greatly drawn to Attic Classicism,
found their inspiration in a post-Classical model which
appealed to them because it was closer to their own imagina-
tive genius.

Iberian pottery, however, is far from being a mere, and
more or less successful, copy of Italiote ceramics. Spanish
vase-painters borrowed no more than they needed. A powerful indigenous tradition led them to intersperse their figures
with certain geometrical elements. Their fondness for curves

of every sort, combined with an extreme aversion for empty spaces, made them fill every available gap with fantastic volutes. They stylised all their representations so completely that the starting-point is often hard to recognise, especially in the case of plant motifs.

The treatment of human and animal figures, although sometimes allowing of a certain realism, is also affected by this stylisation. This again may be attributed to the artist's real or supposed lack of skill. But as we have seen in the case of sculpture, it can be interpreted by the fact that the artist was simply seeking to convey certain scenes, actions or objects clearly, without the Greek painter's concern for realistic representation. As we see, the path taken by Iberian vase-painters led them a long way from their models.

The south-eastern style

It was probably at the very end of the fourth century that pottery with figures first appeared in the south-eastern region. It flourished during the third century and it certainly lasted until the first. The dates are still subject to much discussion;

78 La Albufereta (Alicante). Kalathos. Height 17 cm.
(Provincial Archaeological Museum, Alicante)
*79 La Escuera (San Fulgencio, Alicante). Oenochoe.
Third century. Height 25 cm.* (Provincial Archaeological
Museum, Alicante)

this, however, is a question which would take us too far
afield. Many centres in this region produced figured pottery,
but naturally the most interesting collections of well-preserved
vases were found in the great necropolei, in particular
Verdolay (Cabecico del Tesoro), El Cigarralejo and Archena.
The style of the two latter centres is so closely related to that
of Elche that archaeologists frequently speak of the school of
Elche-Archena.

The Verdolay vases are interesting in that they often display
a transitional style between geometrical and figured pottery,
although this does not mean that they are earlier than the
others. Thus the Alicante museum has a fine urn (fig. 78)
in the form of a *kalathos*. Between the traditional bands
circumscribing the decorated area above and below, we find

a number of concentric circles which may have been painted with a kind of comb revolving on its own axis. Circling the base of the register runs a great foliated scroll with a broad stem, from which heart-shaped (or ivy) leaves branch out, each flanked by upright volutes.

This version of the foliated scroll, probably borrowed from Apulian ceramics, is in itself characteristic of the temperament of the south-eastern vase-painters, with their tendency to exaggerated stylisation. Leaves become spear-heads and volutes are there to fill up the space. The same leaves, surrounded by other foliage of the same type, appear on the charming little jug from La Escuera (San Fulgencio, Alicante) in the same museum (fig. 79).

The division into metopes and the line of spirals are also borrowed from the Mediterranean repertory. Another *kalathos* (fig. 80) offers an instructive comparison and it may represent a development of the earlier one. The foliated scroll

80 El Cabecico del Tesoro (Verdolay, Murcia). Kalathos. *End of third century. Height 18 cm.* (Archaeological Museum, Murcia)

81 El Cabecico del Tesoro (Verdolay, Murcia). Kalathos. *End of third century. Height 15·5 cm.* (Archaeological Museum, Murcia)

82 El Cabecico del Tesoro (Verdolay, Murcia). Large oenochoe. End of third century. Height 37·5 cm. (Archaeological Museum, Murcia)

consists of three parallel lines, the two outer ones being the result of a stylisation of the leaf-stems. The leaf is inverted at the centre of the curve, the volutes hanging down over the circles at the bottom end in spirals, and the painter has suddenly taken advantage of the space left him to add a couple of eyes which turn the whole thing into a grimacing or laughing face like something in a picture puzzle. We hope of course that this was not meant to be a portrait of the deceased! Those who used the vessel, however, are unlikely to have noticed what strikes us today as amusing. The remaining meanders are filled up with birds, obvious funerary symbols, and with more foliage.

A third example shows the same stylisation carried a stage further. The space is even more completely filled. New elements have been introduced, such as a fish and a sign which may represent the shore or the earth, although the precise meaning of their funerary symbolism escapes us (fig. 81). The heart-shaped leaf, surrounded by its double volutes, is easily recognisable. To understand the elements surrounding the fish one must turn to the back of the vase (pl. VIb). Here we find four stems springing from triangles based on two vertical bands which are not seen in the photograph. These stems carry four trumpet-shaped flowers, patterned with hatchings and zigzags, and ending in a spiral.

If we turn to the other side, we see clearly that the fish is placed between the same trumpet-shaped flowers in a much elongated form, and we find them again on the 'carnassier' (wild beast) vase (pl. VIa). This is all fairly simple. The construction is harder to follow on the great *oenochoe* in the Murcia museum (fig. 82), since here the draughtsmanship is less precise. Within two great loops we can make out the two long petals of the flower, this time enclosing a spiral. At the end of each loop there is a stylised flower-bud akin to the forms of the Elche-Archena school.

We find these yet again on the 'carnassier' vase, from Verdolay, on a fine foliated scroll and at the tips of a trumpet-

83 *El Cabecico del Tesoro* (*Verdolay,*   171
Murcia). '*Goat' vase. End of third century.*
Height 25·5 cm. (Archaeological Museum,
Murcia)

shaped flower closely akin to the classic model of the lotus
flower. But the important elements here are the two wild
animals which take up the whole of the upper register. They
are hard to identify, having wolf-like heads and bodies but
the claws of birds or griffins. Their function is unquestionably
to protect the dead.

The 'goat vase' (fig. 83) further enriches our repertory of
symbols; as well as fishes and birds, we find an enigmatic
figure (which is also seen on the vases of Liria) placed
between the two fishes: it seems to be a stylised version of that
delicate aquatic insect, the water-boatman, and must

therefore be considered as one of the symbols of water. The
goats, drawn almost realistically in silhouette, also anticipate
the vase-paintings of Liria. Stylised versions of the two themes
are transposed on another *kalathos* from Verdolay (fig. 84).

In the ceramic ware of Archena, to the north of Murcia
and Elche, stylisation becomes even more linear, with larger
elements in admirably balanced compositions. The painters
of this school show a liking for metopes on the body or neck
of their vases (figs. 85, 86 and 87) while maintaining the
habitual division into superimposed registers. Fantastic
animals which may perhaps have influenced the imaginary
fauna of Verdolay – as instanced in the great *kalathos* from
Murcia – sometimes take up almost the entire surface of the

84 *El Cabecico del Tesoro (Verdolay, Murcia)*. Kalathos. *Third or second century. Height 21 cm.* (Archaeological Museum, Murcia)

85 *El Cabezo de Tio Pio (Archena, Murcia)*. Pithos. *Third century.* (Archaeological Museum, Barcelona)

86 *La Alcudia (Elche, Alicante)*. *Cylindrical vase. Third or second century. Height 16 cm.* (Municipal Museum, Elche)

vase. The rest of the space is filled by the customary plant motifs.

Similar decoration is found on a *pithos* in the Barcelona museum (fig. 85). The animal in the metope is a rudimentary 'winged wild beast', its function being to protect the dead person whose ashes were contained in the great urn. The space here has been filled up with cunningly spiralled flower-buds, a heart-shaped leaf with asymmetrical append-ages to fill the gaps and by an eight-petalled rosette. But the Elche pottery is above all rich in religious significance.

The great eagle on the *pithos* in the museum at La Alcudia has undoubtedly a funerary function, but the most surprising thing is that it seems to produce plant forms, such as ivy leaves and other foliage, which emerge from its wings. The eagle on the cylindrical vase in the Municipal Museum of Elche (fig. 86) is perhaps merely a hypostasis of the great goddess depicted on the *pithos* of the museum of La Alcudia (fig. 87). She is presumably ruling over the kingdom of the dead as she stands between two different plant patterns (on the right we can see an eagle on the trumpet-shaped flower). The symmetry of this design is by no means absolute for there are rosettes on one side of the figure and buds on the other. The schematic treatment of the dress recurs elsewhere, notably on the Liria vases. The student of Iberian sculpture will readily recognise the necklaces at the top of the figure and the underskirt at its foot.

The relationship between the winged goddess and birds is also evident on the great *oenochoe* in the museum at Elche (fig. 20), where she appears on the neck of the vase. She also seems to be associated with snakes and even with a sheep, an animal seldom represented in indigenous art, whether painting or sculpture. Moreover there is some kind of link between the eagles and the snake which is gliding along one of their wings (fig. 21). Despite the diversity of these creatures, they form a fairly coherent group of symbols whose significance has already been explained.

Another aspect of the goddess – unless the figure represents a different deity – is shown on the great jar in the museum of La Alcudia, which is unfortunately severely mutilated. She stands between two great winged horses, spreading out her arms and wings. Her short-sleeved outer garment is fastened by a cord and her small triangular face with its wide-open eyes is seen from the front. This treatment marks a significant advance in the representation of the human face, hitherto always shown in profile. The same full face forms the handle of a vase which has been lost. But is it still the face of the goddess or merely an amusing woman's head, painted for some festive occasion? Or did the head of the goddess become

87 La Alcudia (Elche, Alicante). Detail of a pithos. *Total height of vase 68 cm.* (La Alcudia Museum, Elche)

a mere ornament at some later date, in this case the first century B.C. ?

The answer may be found in the vase known as *la pepona* (the doll) in the museum of La Alcudia, where the head with its painted cheeks, its smoothly parted hair and plaits rises out of a lotus bud which forms the chin (fig. 88). As in the case of the Murcia *kalathos* (fig. 80), it is circumscribed within a space defined not by the curve of a foliated scroll but by that of the handle projecting from the side of the vase. Although the goddess's figure appears in this same position on a cylindrical vase, the two painted heads should perhaps

88 *La Alcudia* (*Elche, Alicante*). 'La pepona' vase. Handled kalathos. *Second century.* (La Alcudia Museum, Elche)

be identified as masks of the deceased or of votaries. The great *kalathos* of *la pepona* is almost entirely covered with figures of protective animals, eagles and wild beasts. They are combined with floral motifs which issue from their bodies and wings.

On a *kalathos* from Archena, in the Madrid museum, we see one of the few examples of the portrayal of horsemen in south-eastern vase-painting. Its style suggests that of Liria which possibly influenced it. The horse is rearing above the body of the warrior whom the rider has just killed with his lance. The treatment, unusual in Archena, half-way between linear drawing and silhouette, also includes geometrical elements: waves and stars, which are schematised rosettes. The funerary significance of this scene is obvious.

The Liria vases

El Cerro de San Miguel, the hill which overlooks the little town of Liria, 25 kilometres to the north-west of Valencia, was the site of an Iberian town which has already been mentioned. A substantial quantity of pottery has been extracted from the dwellings here: plates, *kalathoi*, *oenochoai*, *pithoi* and handleless *kraters*. As is usually the case with pottery found in dwellings, these vases were in a fragmentary condition, although not so badly damaged as those of Elche. Some of them moreover had been broken when the roofs collapsed and were burnt brown by the fire that destroyed the town. This accounts for the dark colour of certain sherds in the reconstituted vases.

Their decoration ranges from the purely geometric (wavy lines, rings, zigzags and so on) to the representation of figures. But whereas at Elche and at Archena flower and animal forms predominated, at Liria there are more representations of human beings. This pottery is clearly of enormous interest for our knowledge of Iberian religion and society. A patient study of the magnificent collection in the Museum of Prehistory at Valencia reveals a whole series of ritual scenes, religious symbols, scenes of battle and fighting animals, depicted in a most lifelike fashion. All the details have been noted by archaeologists from Valencia, led by D. Fletcher, in the *corpus* of the Liria vases.

Several problems arise. For one thing, what were these vases used for? As L. Pericot has suggested, this pottery was probably a luxury article for the inhabitants of Liria, if we contrast the huge pile of undecorated potsherds with the few hundred finely made vases found in the site. Yet one can distinguish clear stylistic differences in the Liria vases. Those which convey the most careful workmanship are covered with linear drawings, the details of face or dress being more or less realistically portrayed within the contour of the figure. On others the figures are merely silhouetted, and much less skilfully than those painted on the 'goat vase'. In some instances the drawing is extremely naïve, though of remarkable aesthetic quality. The question of whether one type of vase was earlier than the other has arisen, but has not yet been satisfactorily answered.

Certain Greek objects found here, to which a reliable date has been ascribed, prove that there was already a small Iberian town at San Miguel in the fourth century B.C. But the fragments of pottery found which were used at that time were either plain or geometrically decorated. The representation of figures, including those of human beings, did not develop fully until the beginning or first half of the third century B.C.

One of the earliest vases of Liria may have been that cylindrical pot, decorated solely with plant motifs, which naïvely transcribes certain motifs of late Greek vase-painting, especially the elongated palmettes drawn upside down (pl. VIc). But the most interesting feature is the great central flower, an adaptation of the lotus flower or *fleur-de-lis*, in which we can recognise the prototype of our trumpet-shaped flowers.

A higher degree of stylisation is shown on a *kalathos*, probably of a later date, where the decoration is divided

179

89 Cerro de San Miguel (Liria, Valencia). Detail from a handleless krater. Third century. Total height of vase 36 cm. External diameter 55 cm. (Museum of Prehistory, Valencia)

90 Cerro de San Miguel (Liria, Valencia). Another detail of the vase shown in fig. 89

into metopes. In each of these the fillets surrounding the central leaf end up as fantastic animals carrying pomegranates at the tip of their trunks. They may perhaps represent seahorses, here replacing the fishes or water-boatmen of the other vases as symbols of water.

Among the articles of simple workmanship with silhouetted figures is an amusing handleless *krater* entirely illustrated with easily recognisable fighting scenes. On the first (fig. 89) a wild boar is being attacked by dogs. The painter has resorted to artifice to differentiate the various animals, as the dogs have manes like those of wild boars and the boar has a head like a dog's; the muzzle has been broadened to suggest a snout, and to make things quite plain the painter has added a corkscrew tail. The significance of the window-like spaces inside the figures escapes us completely. They may perhaps represent the spine and viscera of the animals, shown as it were by X-ray.

The second scene is more complex (fig. 90): a man is taming a horse by beating it, while another rider gallops up. The two triangles decorated with volutes are puzzling. Are they pieces of harness? Dogs are looking on, one barking, another scratching himself nonchalantly. The whole thing, crude as it is, echoes the themes of Greek painting: the horseman holding his mount by its bridle, the domestic dogs that lie at the feet of reclining feasters in banquet scenes. The painter has combined the two in a curious fashion.

An eagle, swooping down head-first towards the right, leads us on to the second scene (fig. 91) that represents the capture or killing of a bull. The two *toreros* are holding weapons which have been variously explained. The final scene depicts a strange and bloodthirsty battle. Two men in helmets protect themselves with concave shields. The warrior on the left, brandishing his *falcata*, has already flung his spear and wounded his adversary whose blood is flowing copiously (fig. 92).

The painting of these scenes, for all its rudimentary

91 Cerro de San Miguel (Liria, Valencia). Another detail of the vase shown in fig. 89

92 Cerro de San Miguel (Liria, Valencia). Another detail of the vase shown in fig. 89

character, obeys certain elementary laws which govern most primitive art: the head seen in profile with the eye shown frontally, the frontal trunk and the legs in profile, scant attempts at perspective, the transposition of elements (the animals' manes for instance) which shift from one figure to another taking on a different meaning. We shall find these characteristics in all the Liria vase-paintings, even the most sophisticated.

Nevertheless these silhouette painters are often adept at conveying movement and detail. On another vase from Liria, depicting a stag-hunting scene, the rider is drawn as one piece with his horse (fig. 93). Anyone looking at it, even if he is not struck by the spontaneous beauty of the drawing, will recognise the violence of the onslaught conveyed by the rider's gesture, and the straining horse with its lolling tongue.

The same comments might be made about the 'Vase with Two Riders', which represents a couple riding side by side; perspective is simply suggested by the relative position of the two silhouettes.

Occasionally both techniques are used on a single vase (fig. 94). The figures are in silhouette, but the two birds dividing a lotus flower are drawn in outline. This outline drawing, with summary suggestions of details inside the figure, had of course to be done before the silhouette was filled in. It also forms a transition to the second style of the Liria vase-painters.

This, whether earlier or later than the style we have just described, represents a combination of all these themes, attitudes and motifs in densely-painted compositions which have sometimes been described as baroque. In fact, despite an undeniable superiority of draughtsmanship, there is often a marked distortion of figures and symbols, all the more noticeable because of the improved technique. Consider, for instance, the scene decorating a large handleless *krater* which shows a fight between two warriors – possibly a ritual contest – in the presence of musicians (fig. 17). The faces are

93 Cerro de San Miguel (Liria, Valencia). Detail from a
pithos. *Third or second century. Diameter of vase 54 cm.*
(Museum of Prehistory, Valencia)

94 Cerro de San Miguel (Liria, Valencia). Detail from a
pithos. *Third or second century. Diameter 45 cm.* (Museum
of Prehistory, Valencia)

mere caricatures and the motifs that fill up the spaces between the figures are highly stylised.

With this second Liria style, we also find a new method of composition, fuller, more continuous and more regular. The painter now needs the full height of the register, for in spite of apparent disorder he is more in control of his space. In the 'Vase of the Dance', the figures are set out thus: four women and three men holding hands, led by two musicians, a woman playing a double flute and a man blowing a horn. The motifs between them are often distorted by the addition of curves or appendages. But the painter has carefully portrayed the dancers' dress. The women are clad in small mitres and long dresses with full underskirts, whereas the men wear helmets with low crests and short tunics with crossover neck openings – clothes which were fashionable in Iberia in the later period.

The most successful example of the second Liria style of vase-painting is undeniably the 'Warrior Vase'. This is similar in composition (fig. 95) and depicts a ritual battle, performed here by foot-soldiers and a charge of mounted spearmen. In spite of the regular distribution of the figures, it gives the impression that they are all in a single line, or possibly two, spaced in a primitive attempt to convey perspective. The careful treatment of the elements used to fill up spaces is striking, as is their variety – foliated scrolls, water-insects, heart-shaped leaves, rosettes and lotus flowers. These are protective symbols, as is shown by their presence on the men's shields. The attacking warrior carries the customary weapons – a spear and a *falcata* – and wears a crested helmet; the novelty here is the scaled cuirass – the Romans' *lorica squamata* – unless it is a coat of mail worn over a short fringed tunic. Short boots and armbands complete his outfit.

The Azaila vases

As has been established by Cabré, the figure-painted pottery of the south-eastern and Valencian schools influenced the beginnings of figure-painted pottery in Aragon, where the

95 *Cerro de San Miguel (Liria, Valencia).*
'Warrior' vase. Handleless krater. *Second or*
first century. Total height 42·5 cm. External
diameter 57·5 cm. (Museum of Prehistory,
Valencia)

most notable site is Cabezo de Alcalá-Azaila. According to
Cabré, these traditions were introduced by the Iberians
when they conquered the Celtic town at the end of the third
century; without completely adhering to this precise opinion,
one must recognise that the vase-painting of Azaila came
into being under the combined influence of Hellenistic
ceramics and of the Iberian pottery of the south-east, after
the Roman conquest.

Its forms are less varied. They comprise chiefly cylindrical
vases with handles and lids, *kalathoi, kraters*, with handles and
hollow dishes. The vase-painters of Azaila took stylisation a
step further by combining and complicating the vegetal
elements, particularly the ivy leaf and the lotus bud. They

covered their vases with a dense pattern of volutes and foils, often emphasised by a slender line. Human figures are scarcer, but there are a great many birds in the Lirian style. Also evident are rampant wild animals – fish, hares and so forth. Some foliated candelabras recall the ancient 'Tree of Life'. They are of course borrowed from Hellenistic painting, as is also the vertical lay-out of the figures in an attempt to convey perspective.

This interesting school of vase-painting lingered on into the first century B.C., but was to be supplanted by the vases with decoration in relief – Italic first, then Gallo-Roman and

Hispanic – which became popular in Iberia at the end of the first century.

The problem of mural painting

The existence of large-scale decorative painting has been postulated by A. García y Bellido, who saw evidence of this in the composition of those vases from Liria and Elche where certain figures are seen full face. One might also cite the mythological scenes on the Tivisa *patera* (fig. 25) which seem to be copied from larger models. But scarcely anything is left of this mural painting, and we cannot even reconstruct

96 Galera (Granada). Stone cist. Sixth century. Height 26 cm. (National Archaeological Museum, Madrid)

its themes since we have no ancient texts to help us, as in the case of pictures by great Greek painters.

One tomb at Galera, however, did show wall paintings with geometrical decorations and figures. On the floor there could be made out six lines, each of four great 'closed palmettes', highly stylised in red, black, yellow and white. The plaster on the walls was covered with scenes of battle or hunting. Unfortunately none of this has survived, for everything was destroyed shortly after its discovery. Cabré had time, however, to record the painting of the floor. The cists in the same necropolis are also sometimes decorated with ritual scenes. Although they are almost obliterated today, on one we can make out a woman praying before a seated goddess. Another, better preserved, has an ornamental band running round it and an interlacing pattern on its lid (fig. 96).

CHAPTER 8
Metalwork
and jewellery

For the writers of antiquity, as we have seen, Spain was primarily the land of metals; these undeniably constituted the principal wealth of the Tartessian region. Yet their writings refer only briefly to the metalworking of the Spaniards, apart from their mining activities. Only Spanish weapons, which had been exported from the Bronze Age onwards, were highly valued by the Romans who considered Spain as a producer of raw materials.

Archaeology has proved, however, that these foreigners' views were too narrow. It has revealed the rich and prolific production of metalwork in Spain, from gold jewellery to silver plate, from bronze statuettes to iron weapons. The quality of these articles presupposes the existence of active crafts and long apprenticeship. If their appearance during the Iberian period was due to foreign influence, they had the advantage of a long previous tradition of metalworking. It is a known fact that as early as the Bronze Age the Spaniards were producing remarkable gold jewellery and a whole panoply of weapons and tools of careful and original workmanship.

Goldsmiths' work

The goldsmiths' craft developed in the Tartessian region and in the south during the Bronze Age, when the civilisation of El Argar produced magnificent diadems, swords with gold-plated pommels, bracelets and even gold plate, examples of which were found in the famous treasure of Villena (Alicante).

Finds of the Iberian period are usually in the form of treasure hoards, sometimes of metal founders' stores or isolated objects. The hoards can be divided into two great geographical groups: those of the Tartessian region and those of the south-east. A third and later group is found in Catalonia. The most famous treasures of the Tartessian group are those of Aliseda (Cáceres), belonging to the seventh and sixth centuries, and of Sanlúcar de Barrameda (Cadiz) and El Carambolo (Seville), both of the sixth century. The collection at Santiago de la Espada (Jaén) is of a somewhat later date, ranging from the fifth to the third centuries.

The most notable of the south-eastern group are the treasures of Jávea (Alicante), fifth and fourth centuries, and the metal founders' store of Cheste (Valencia), sixth to third centuries (fig. 108). The treasures of Catalonia and Aragon belong to the Roman period. That of Tivisa, whose silver plate we shall study later, belongs to the second century, as does the necklace from Serós (Lérida).

Jewellers' techniques

Even more than in other fields of Iberian art, the influence of the East was dominant here from the start. It was no doubt from Eastern craftsmen that the men of El Argar, and later those of Tartessos, learned the technique of smelting gold and silver ores. We have unfortunately no earlier documentation than Strabo's account of the preparation of these precious metals. The nuggets and flakes of gold, he tells us, were melted with 'a kind of earth like alum' to produce an alloy known as electrum, in which gold and silver were mixed. A second melting down in a crucible made possible the separation of the two metals and the casting of the gold into ingots.

Strabo's description of the process is undoubtedly incomplete. The Oriental technique of cupellation through oxidation must already have been used by Spaniards from early times to eliminate inferior metals. It was undoubtedly in order to separate the silver from the gold that 'a kind of earth like alum' was used.

The metal thus obtained, of which Tartessian jewellery was made, has been analysed. It is extremely pure, containing over 90 per cent gold in most cases. This obviously made it easier to work, but reduced the toughness of the articles.

Repoussé work was the earliest technique used by gold-smiths and was employed in the manufacture of the golden bowls of Villena as early as the Bronze Age, and subsequently for all kinds of articles. The gold was first hammered flat into a thin sheet, then laid against a core of soft wood and worked from the wrong side with a wooden punch. The relief thus produced could be repeated on a flat surface, as on the votive lamina from the Museo Valencia de Don Juan (fig. 10), representing a man in a short tunic. Embossing was also used to repeat certain figures on the Aliseda belt.

It was later, probably in the seventh century, that the Tartessians began to use gold thread firstly to make small chains, then for the filigree decoration we find on the jewellery of Cadiz and in that of the treasure hoard of Aliseda, and naturally in the jewellery of later hoards. A technique commonly used in Greece consisted of twisting one, two or three strands together to make a plait which was afterwards soldered to the body of the piece. This was the process used by the goldsmith who made the diadem of Jávea to decorate the terminal triangles.

At the same time the technique of granulation reached southern Iberia and was largely employed for the pieces in the Aliseda hoard and for all jewellery of the archaic and middle periods. Much has been written about this astonishing Oriental invention of the third millennium, which enabled the surface of the ornament to be covered with minute grains to create a matt background contrasting with the brilliance of the jewels set, or lines producing an effect like filigree (fig. 98).

Metalwork and jewellery

The difficulty we find today in reproducing this process in the laboratory increases our admiration for the Iberian goldsmiths who had such primitive means at their disposal. Although the Iberians' granules were never as fine as those in Etruscan jewellery, there was the same problem of soldering them to the background of the ornament; this was the great disadvantage of the process. It is generally believed today that the jewellers of antiquity used an adhesive with a resin and copper oxide base, but we are still uncertain as to the method used.

Finally the Iberians practised soldering with gold, pure or alloyed, to join the small plaques, threads and plaits to the body of the ornaments. This may have been the most difficult part of the process, since soldering with gold requires a precise degree of heat. It must be admitted that they were not always as successful as their Greek or Oriental masters, but this is seldom visible to the naked eye. The archaeologist may be grateful for this weakness, which enables him the better to distinguish imported objects from their local imitations.

In the making of the finest ornaments, of which only two or three specimens have been found in the Peninsula, all these techniques were clearly used in combination. The Aliseda diadem (fig. 97) is the product of remarkably skilled craftsmanship. It consists in the first place of a set of gold plaques joined with tubular hinges, which can be seen at the back of the piece, and of small chains ending in granules. The decoration of the central elements consists of two gold threads soldered on to a row of granules rolled spirally round a tiny cup to form a rosette. These cuplets were filled with coloured glass beads in the Phoenician tradition (pl. VIIIa). On the two terminal triangles, rows of granules form the pattern of the large lotus flower and the rosette, while in the angles smaller flowers stand out against a granulated background (fig. 98).

97 *Aliseda (Cáceres). Diadem. Seventh century. Total length 20 cm.* (National Archaeological Museum, Madrid)

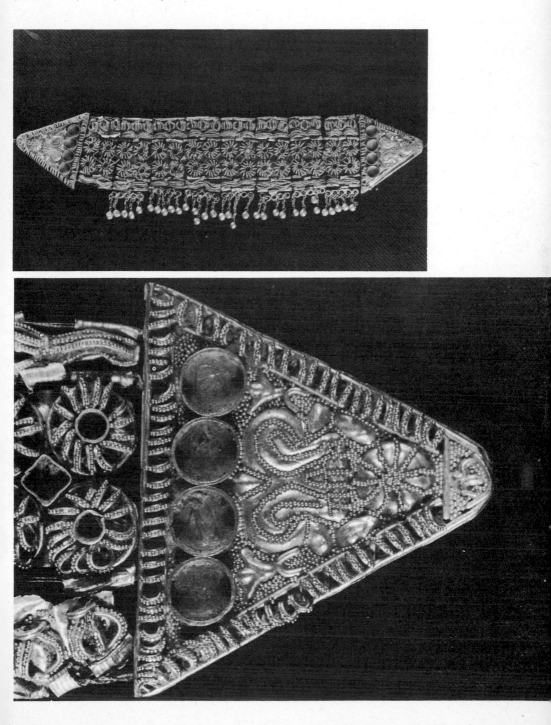

98 *Aliseda (Cáceres). Detail from diadem*

The themes of Iberian jewellery

Iberian jewellery, quite apart from its exceptional quality and abundance, provides a rewarding study for the archaeologist and the art historian. It comprises a repertory of iconographic themes borrowed from the Orient and from Greece and it is a precious source of information about Iberian religious practices, society and daily life. Furthermore, by consulting the representation of these ornaments on sculptured figures we can sometimes ascribe them unmistakably to a specific social category.

Purely geometrical themes are scarcer in Iberia than in the Celtic regions of Spain. The most common motifs are those taken from plant life. For instance we find spirals (or more exactly spiralling S's) on the bracelet from Aliseda between two rows of double braids (fig. 99).

The Jávea diadem also shows geometrical patterns which, in spite of the Greek filigree technique, betray its indigenous origin: large meanders, tiny zigzags, diamond shapes with eyes and so on. But the main part of the decoration is vegetal: the great foliated scrolls and the row of ivy leaves pointing upwards, the *fleurs-de-lis* inverted by their S-shaped bases or placed one above the other as in the terminal triangles.

The rosette, which we saw in the Aliseda diadem, is used in many other ornaments such as in the plaques from Carambolo, where it is treated in repoussé, and the earpendants from the hoard of Santiago de la Espada (fig. 107), where the petals are partitioned as in *cloisonné*. The palmette is even more widely used: there is a charming necklace of embossed palmettes in the Aliseda hoard. They are treated with characteristic Iberian exuberance on certain bracelets, the ends of which are made up of one large palmette whose petals consist of three smaller ones against a granular background (fig. 100).

Vegetal themes are also combined in a small ear-pendant from Estremadura (fig. 101), the rim of which consists of small

99 Aliseda (Cáceres). Detail from the centre of a bracelet. Seventh century. Width of band 20 mm. Diameter 60–66 mm. (National Archaeological Museum, Madrid)

100 Aliseda (Cáceres). Terminal ornamentation of the bracelet

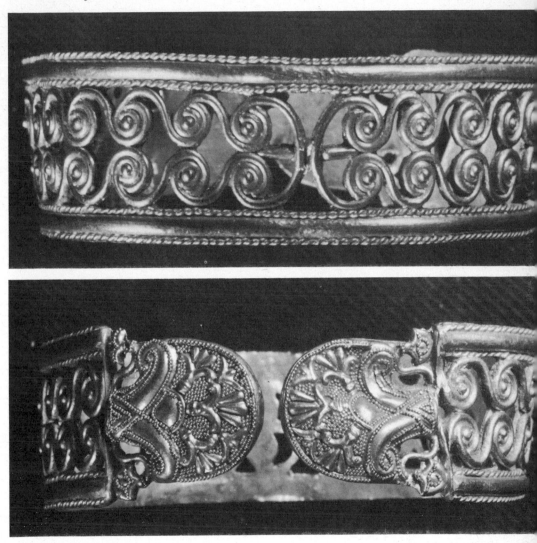

open flowers resting on closed lotus flowers separated by palmettes.

The ear-pendant from Aliseda, in which the first animal motifs appear, is a magnificent piece weighing not less than 35 grammes (fig. 102). A small chain went round the ear to relieve the pierced lobe of the rich lady who wore it. The rim is an elaborate composition of lotus flowers, trumpet-shaped

flowers and palmettes, with eagles perched among them. This is the earliest representation of an assemblage which, as we have seen, recurs four centuries later on Iberian pottery.

On sheaths for amulets from Cadiz (fig. 103), we recognise the attributes of Egyptian deities in the shape of animals' heads crowned with a solar disk: Sekhmet (lioness), Khnoum (ram) and Horus (falcon). Although later than the Aliseda treasure, these pieces constitute an important landmark between the Orientalising art of the Mediterranean and Iberian art: it was the diffusion of small objects such as these that resulted in the creation of fantastic animals by sculptors and vase-painters.

The finest of the three reconstructed necklaces from Aliseda may have played a similar role (fig. 13). As well as curious crescent-shaped elements, it includes amulet-containers with

101 Estremadura. Ear-pendant. Seventh or sixth century. External diameter 77 mm. (National Archaeological Museum, Madrid)

102 Aliseda (Cáceres). Gold ear-pendant. External diameter 7·6 cm. (National Archaeological Museum, Madrid)

falcons' heads (fig. 104) directly borrowed from Phoenicia or Carthage and serpents' heads between two spheroids.

The belt from the same treasure enriches our knowledge of the fantastic fauna of Iberian mythology and its decorative or protective function. Made up of gold plaques and a gold band sewn on to a leather belt, with two separate plaques forming a clasp (fig. 105), all the various techniques are employed here, except filigree. The sumptuous buckle has at its centre those closed palmettes, probably of Cypriot origin, which we have seen elsewhere. The motif of a man

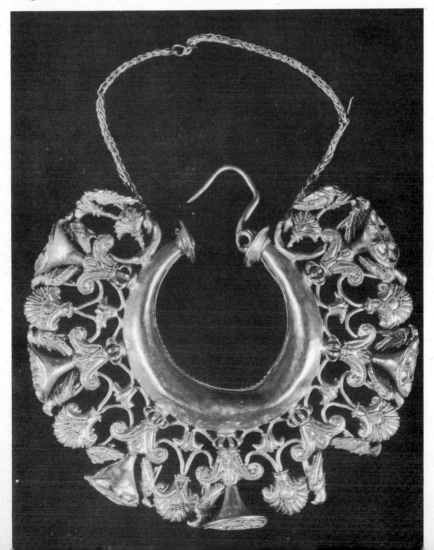

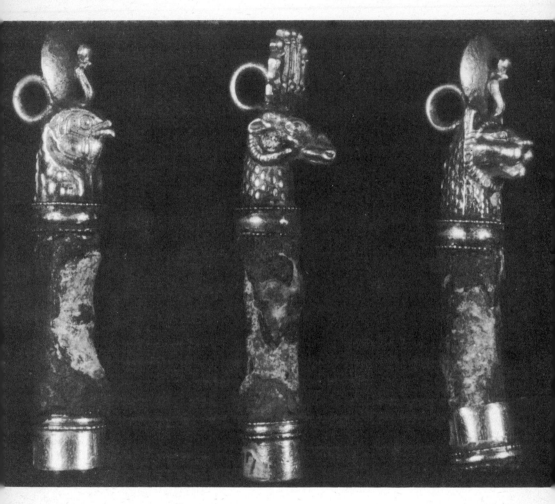

taming a lion, from whose tail the Tree of Life springs up, is depicted on its border (fig. 106) recurring in the centre of the belt amid a row of griffins.

Scarabs mounted on seals with swivelling mounts also played an important part in the diffusion of Oriental themes. One scene depicts worshippers on either side of a pillar surmounted by a closed palmette representing the Tree of Life (pl. VIIIc), underneath a large vulture with outspread wings. The Aliseda treasure has a series of such rings with swivelling mounts, in which the scarabs are engraved with

103 Gold and bronze sheaths for amulets. Fifth century. Height 40 mm. (Provincial Archaeological Museum, Cadiz)

104 Aliseda (Cáceres). Amulet sheath from necklace in fig. 13. Height 4·2 cm.

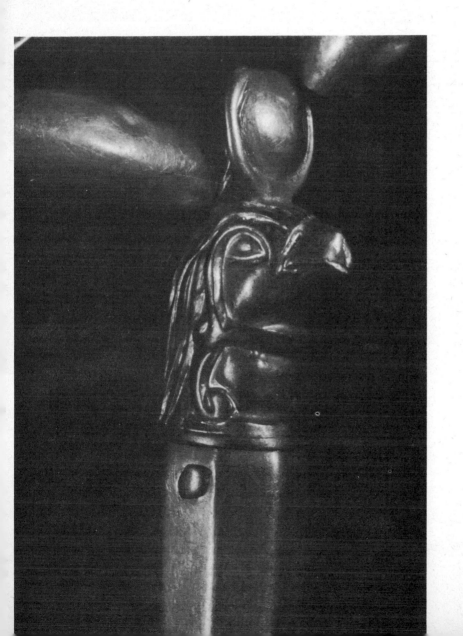

105 Aliseda (Cáceres). Gold sword-belt.
Seventh century. Overall length 82 cm.
(National Archaeological Museum,
Madrid)

106 Aliseda (Cáceres). Detail from the gold
sword-belt

religious emblems which have enriched our knowledge of Iberian iconography.

One of these scarabs, made of jasper, is decorated with the figure of a votary holding a banner in his left hand and raising an outsize right hand in greeting. A. Blanco attributes a Syrian origin to this. Another scarab (pl. VIIIb), in agate, portrays a winged figure with two heads.

The goddess who appears on the ear-pendant from Santiago de la Espada (fig. 107) takes us back to the motifs we saw on the Elche vases. She has small wings behind her head. The treatment of the veil or cloak suggests the wings of an Oriental demon. J. Cabré has pointed out the resemblance of her dress and her long plaits to those of the statuettes from Despeñaperros, one of which carries the same bird either as a divine attribute or as an offering. Here however the right hand is pouring a libation from a small *patera*.

All this iconography is known to have a magical significance. Were these emblems intended to serve a protective purpose or simply to create a harmonious composition? The Iberians had probably not as yet come to use them for a purely decorative purpose, and we shall see how much superstition still clung to them.

Silver work

Even in the rich land of Spain, gold was rarer than silver, and, according to E. Cuadrado, four times as valuable. Silver was produced abundantly in the interior, and was sometimes mingled with gold ore but more frequently with lead. It served as raw material for a whole series of treasures, mostly later than those already described, ranging from the fourth century to the Roman conquest. We may mention those of Torre de Juan Abad (Ciudad Real), Los Almadenes de Pozoblanco (Cordoba), Santisteban del Puerto (Jaén), Mogón (Jaén), Salvacañete (Cuenca) and Tivisa (Tarragona).

107 Santiago de la Espada (Jaén). Detail of ear-pendant. Height of figurine 3·6 cm. Total height 10 cm. (Valencia de Don Juan Museum, Madrid)

108 Cheste (Valencia). Torque and silver fibula pin

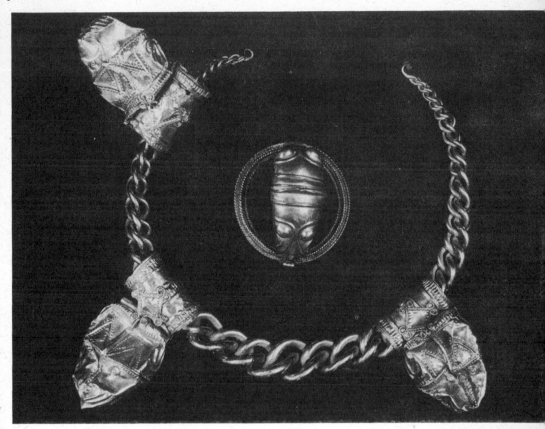

Silver jewellery

Although produced in Iberian territory, a great many ornaments and other silver objects show Celtic influence as also do certain gold ornaments, such as the small plaque from the Museo Valencia de Don Juan (fig. 10), the torque and the fibula-pin from the treasure at Cheste (fig. 108), the bow of which is formed from two heads facing opposite ways – a theme which recurs elsewhere; for instance, in the medallion in repoussé work from the treasure of Los Almadenes de Pozoblanco (fig. 24) in the Cordoba museum. The Cheste fibula, however, is in the usual shape of Hispanic annular fibula.

These silver articles, with others of more definitely Celtic

character, raise the question of Celtic penetration into the
Tartessian and Iberian regions; but we shall not attempt
to discuss this here. If this use of Celtic ornamentation and
techniques can be explained by direct contact in such
marginal sites as Torre de Juan Abad, Mogón or Salvacañete,
it is more unexpected at Los Almadenes de Pozoblanco.

Some scholars have been so much struck by these Celtic
elements in Iberian art that they have unhesitatingly attributed to the Celts a disproportionate role in the formation
of that art. My opinion is that these mingled influences are
chiefly due to the after-effects of the disturbances experienced
by Spain during the third century B.C.

A first group of original works consists of silver plaques and
medallions in repoussé. These are sometimes unimportant
objects (such as those in fig. 24), decorated with rays or
winged insects. More definitely Iberian and of higher artistic

109 Mogón (Jaén). Silver plaque. Third century. Length 15·6 cm.
(National Archaeological Museum, Madrid)

110 Perotito (Santisteban del Puerto, Jaén). Detail of silver bracelet.
First century. (National Archaeological Museum, Madrid)

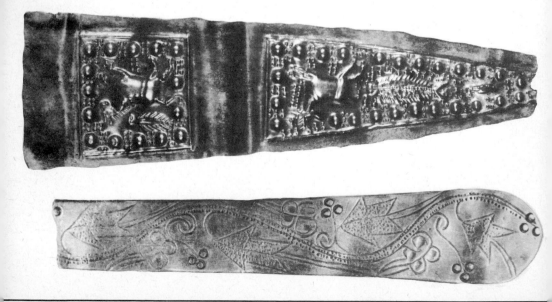

111 Perotito (Santisteban del Puerto, Jaén). Silver chalice. First century. Total height 21 cm. (National Archaeological Museum, Madrid)

merit is the silver plaque from a dagger sheath found at Mogón (fig. 109) which is decorated with animal symbols: deer, fish, birds and horses. The square section depicts a galloping horse beneath a monstrous animal which is part bird and part fish, and the pattern surrounding it echoes architectural elements. This piece may be fourth century.

Silver ornaments were frequently embossed, a method of decoration which their massive character made possible. A curious example is the piece of a bracelet (fig. 110) from Santisteban del Puerto, with its naïve interpretation of the vine tendril motif, possibly inspired by the decoration on a cup in the same hoard which is of Roman workmanship (fig. 111).

*112 Los Almadenes de Pozoblanco (?) (Cordoba). Silver
zoomorphic fibula. Second century. Length 8·7 cm.* (National
Archaeological Museum, Madrid)

Silver fibula-pins showing Celtic influence are often of great
value and the hoard of Pozoblanco has yielded many of a type
midway between the Mediterranean and Celtic forms. All
introduce the horse motif, either in the form of a horse's
head or the figure of a rider, sometimes forming the actual
bow of the fibula (fig. 112).

This particular piece may represent a hunting scene,
although the quarry, seen on the right, is difficult to identify.
The animals are decorated with eye-shapes, chevrons and
double lines which are somewhat puzzling. The technique of
zigzag engraving is found on bracelets in the same hoard
which go back in style to the Bronze Age. Others seem to be
derived from the torque, such as the fine specimen from
Santisteban del Puerto (probably third century) in which the
ends form a sort of Herculean knot (fig. 113).

However, most of these silver bracelets are solenoidal in
form, terminating in a snake's head ornament. This motif is

113 *Perotito (Santisteban del Puerto, Jaén). Silver bracelet.*
Third century. (National Archaeological Museum,
Madrid)

114 *Mengíbar (Jaén). Silver bracelets. Second century.*
Diameter about 7 cm. (National Archaeological Museum,
Madrid)

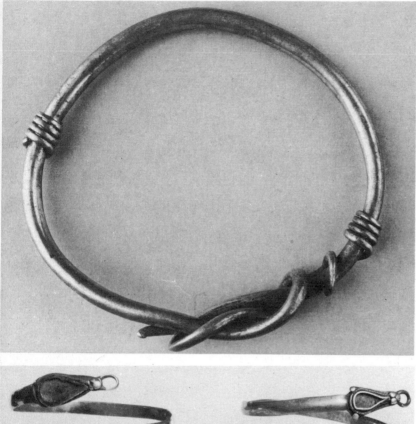

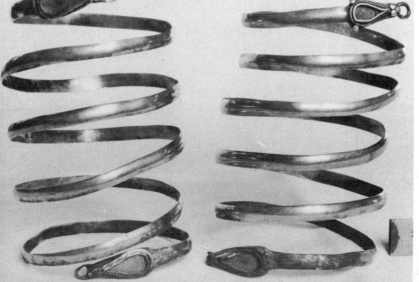

not new, for we find examples dating from the Bronze Age.
On a specimen from Cabrera de Mataró the head is that of a
cobra, freely interpreted by the silversmith. Sometimes the
snake's head has been stylised to provide a mount for a stone
or a glass bead (fig. 114). This technique was also employed
on the bronze fibula-pins of Cigarralejo.

The finest Iberian torques are composed of two or three
twisted strands and are often terminated by eyelets through
which a lace was threaded. It has been quite convincingly
suggested that they were worn by Iberian women, as we see
on certain Oretanian bronzes (fig. 58 and pl. IIId) and sculptures from El Cerro de los Santos (fig. 14). The torque

*115 Perotito (Santisteban del Puerto, Jaén). Silver torque.
Third century.* (National Archaeological Museum,
Madrid)

209

*116 Tivisa (Tarragona). Silver vase. Second century.
Height 9·8 cm.* (Archaeological Museum, Barcelona)

illustrated here (fig. 115) bears no relation to the necklace
depicted on these statues. However, the great twisted necklaces
of Jávea were undoubtedly women's ornaments.

Silver ware and silver plate

Almost all the hoards of Iberian or Ibero-Roman silver have
yielded fine collections of silver dishes, plain, with repoussé
decoration or plated with gold. Naturally the plain, smooth
ware is the most common. Shapes are simple and sometimes
borrowed from pottery: hemispheric bowls, conical cups,
paterae and plates with a central boss, of Classical or Hellenistic type.

Among these elementary shapes, special mention must be
made of the silver strainers of the Roman period, perforated

in rose or star-shaped patterns, in swastikas or ivy-tendrils, recalling the decoration on native pottery. These must justly be described as Ibero-Roman. The Tivisa treasure contained a certain number of carinated vases with splayed necks, a shape which by then had been traditional for the past thousand years. Most of these vases are smooth, but one of them (fig. 116), in the Barcelona museum, is finely decorated in repoussé with vitruvian scrolls, plaits and a series of drop-like figures which can be recognised as acorns and palm-tree hearts.

Paterae treated in repoussé are of finer quality. We have

117 Perotito (Santisteban del Puerto, Jaén). Silver patera. 211
First century. External diameter 17·5 cm. (National
Archaeological Museum, Madrid)

118 Tivisa (Tarragona). Silver patera. *Second century.*
External diameter 15·3 cm. (Archaeological Museum,
Barcelona)

some interesting specimens, imported or made locally by
Greek artists, which may have served as models for the indigenous *paterae* made by the same technique, but with a
different iconography. This is the case with the *patera* of
Hellenistic workmanship from Santisteban del Puerto in the
Madrid museum; its centre depicts the infant Hercules
strangling the serpents and the main part of the dish contains
a series of male and female centaurs, dancers and musicians
(fig. 117). The rim is decorated with a vitruvian scroll of
gold plate. Compared with this, a *patera* from Tivisa in the
Barcelona museum seems to be a native copy of Greek or

Roman work (fig. 118). Yet another, which is of very careful workmanship, is indigenous both in technique and in decoration. A handsome foliated scroll with three volutes has been appliquéd in gold in the centre, with fish and other emblems freely scattered around.

Two other *paterae* from the same treasure are typically indigenous and both have considerable religious importance. The first (fig. 119), with its wolf's or carnivore's head, recalls the warrior's baldric from Elche (fig. 42). Here again we may assume the influence of Hellenistic models, if we compare this *patera* with an embossed medallion from the Barcelona museum.

The second *patera* is a masterpiece of gold plating (fig. 25). In the centre is the head of a roaring lioness. Figures from mythological scenes, which we have studied in chapter 4, are treated in chased silver-gilt. The design is wholly indigenous, but includes the line of wave-moulding along the rim which we have already seen on the *patera* of Santisteban del Puerto (fig. 117).

Belt buckles of inlaid bronze

Belts and buckles featured prominently in men's and women's dress. We have seen for instance what luxury was lavished on the swordbelt from Aliseda. Southern or 'Tartessian' buckles were often made of cast bronze, which were fretted and embossed, and decorated with griffins, or else of leather with ornamental rosettes. They included large hooks with which to fasten the belt.

The buckles of Upper Andalusia, those of Despeñaperros in particular, show strong Celtic influence, as J. Cabré has pointed out. One of these, no doubt an offering from an Iberian mercenary, was discovered in the sanctuary of Olympia at the beginning of this century. The finest of the Despeñaperros buckles are made up of two plaques, of which one, swallow-tail in shape, is connected by a flat hook to the other.

119 Tivisa (Tarragona). Silver patera.
Second century. External diameter 15·3 cm.
(Archaeological Museum, Barcelona)

213

As a rule they were decorated by the damascening process, which was particularly prized by the Spanish Celts and which has remained a live industry in Spain until present times. It involved lightly hollowing out the plaque to be decorated, then applying a sheet of gold or silver leaf by means of a wooden tool or a hammer. The result was most striking. The buckle from Despeñaperros, now in the Madrid museum, which was inlaid with gold in this fashion, is decorated with the wave-mouldings, volutes and ivy tendrils with which we are by now familiar. The Celtic origin formerly ascribed to these designs is nowadays open to question.

Metalwork
and jewellery

Iberian weapons

The same technique was often used to ornament the pommels and scabbards of Iberian weapons. But these deserve a closer study than can be attempted here. The finest were discovered in the necropolis of the Meseta and in others such as Almedinilla (Cordoba) in the south-east, in the south and above all in El Cigarralejo, where E. Cuadrado came across an extremely valuable collection of daggers, swords and weapons of every sort, the study of which has been profitable for our understanding of the problems of influence and chronology. Iberian weapons, famous throughout antiquity, are represented by many types which fall into various groups.

On the one hand there are the short weapons: daggers with broad triangular incised blades, with antenniform hilts – that is to say, with two splayed-out appendages – or with two knobs which form atrophied antennae, or else with a semi-circular pommel. Quite often they are represented on Oretanian bronzes (fig. 60).

The same is true of the long sword which may be the famous *gladius hispaniensis* like the one brandished by the warrior of Osuna (fig. 72). Some Spanish archaeologists however believe that the *gladius* which the Romans admired so much is identical with the typical Iberian *falcata*. This was a curved sword for close fighting, 40 to 60 centimetres in length, featuring a silver hilt inlaid with niello, at first in the form of a bird's head and later of a horse's head, as we see in the fine specimen from Almedinilla in the Madrid museum (fig. 120).

The *falcata* is copiously represented on bronzes (pl. I and IIIc and figs. 8, 9 etc.) and in stone statuary. Curved swords were not unknown in Classical Greece and this has been suggested as the origin of the *falcata*. It may be thought, however, that blades of this shape resulted from an indigenous development of the large curved cutlasses used in Spain from ancient times.

120 *Almedinilla (Cordoba).* Falcata *in iron
and damascened bronze.* Fourth or third
century. Total length *57 cm.* (National
Archaeological Museum, Madrid)

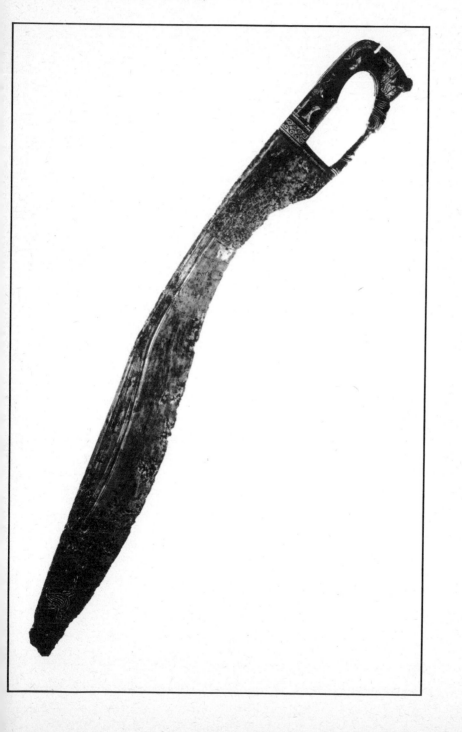

Spanish throwing weapons were almost as famous as Spanish swords. Particularly celebrated were the *soliferrea*, those formidable iron lances against which shields were of little avail, as is illustrated on a vase from Liria (fig. 92). Many have been found at Almedinilla, and the small bronze figures of warriors are sometimes shown holding them (figs. 5 and 62). But Iberian warriors also used *pila*, thousands of which were discovered by Pierre Paris at Osuna, and the *falarica*, a lighter javelin with a wooden handle.

Bucklers were invariably of some light material – leather, wood or fibre – only the central boss being of metal. The Iberians used the *caetra*, or round buckler, either convex or concave in front, which the Oretanian bronze figures carry slung over their backs (figs. 5 and 9, pl. IIIc). The long shield appears on the Osuna reliefs (fig. 72) and on some of the small bronzes. Cuirasses, such as the one worn by the Elche warrior (fig. 42), and greaves were very rare.

Helmets were more commonly, though by no means generally, worn. The Oretanian bronzes and the warriors of Osuna wear Iberian helmets, either crested (pl. I) or round, some of which may merely have been leather caps. The influence of Greek helmets on these native models is unmistakable, as the Greek specimens found at Jerez and Huelva testify.

Hammersmiths' work

The making of bronze vessels by beating the metal – a technique which might be described as hammersmiths' work – was one of the great Iberian specialities, and has been maintained by Spaniards to this day. Yet it was not a native invention, having come into existence in the Tartessian region under Greek and Oriental influence.

The earliest articles thus made were bronze pitchers – pear-shaped *oenochoai* – of which a complete study has been made by A. García y Bellido. They have been found throughout the 'Tartessian' region to such an extent that they virtually define its limits: Lower Andalusia, Estremadura, and Western Castile. They were copied from Cypriot and Oriental models of which a few imported specimens have been discovered. Their main originality lies in the handles which are joined to the neck of the jug with a serpent's head and to the body with an inverted palmette. Some are even surmounted by stags' or panthers' heads and were made in the Peninsula from the seventh to the fifth centuries B.C.

To conclude our study of this archaeological material, let us mention what is perhaps the most Spanish of all these objects – a bronze basin, which was found (accompanied by an *oenochoe*) at Carmona. This shallow bowl with a broad flat border decorated with rosettes in relief, above which the handles are fastened, is similar in shape to the *braseros* used in the countryside of southern Spain. The handles are joined on in the shape of arms following the curve of the rim, like the protective arms that Egyptian goddesses spread over the world of the dead and the living. Bronze basins were among the objects left in the graves in the cremation tumulus of El Cigarralejo in Andalusia. They were made between the seventh and fourth centuries B.C.

The rapid inventory drawn up here of the archaeological evidence bequeathed by Iberian civilisation enables us to appreciate its richness and diversity. The material richness of the objects and the richness of their decoration are due to a long tradition and to the inventive spirit of their creators who assimilated foreign influences. The diversity of artistic disciplines, techniques and inspiration took shape differently in the two great provinces of Iberia, namely the Tartessian and Turdetanian regions on the one hand and the region that extends from the south-east to Catalonia on the other, with further variations within each of these areas, according to even narrower divisions, which we have only begun to recognise today.

All this enables us to measure the inadequacy of written texts as against archaeological evidence for the understanding of a civilisation of this kind. An ever-growing number of discoveries accentuate the contrast and illuminate or correct the assertions of ancient writers. The zones of shadow are slowly dwindling. It is our hope that this study may have helped towards the understanding of what is known today about Iberian art and civilisation.

Bibliography

Recent or important works on Iberian art and civilisation

JOURNALS

Ampurias, Archivo Español de Arqueología, Archivo de Prehistoria levantina, Madrider Mitteilungen, Noticiario Arqueológico Hispánico, Trabajos de Prehistoria, Zephyrus.

GENERAL

A. García y Bellido. *Iberische Kunst in Spanien*. Mainz, 1971.

G. Lilliu, H. Schubart. *Frühe Randkulturen des Mittelmeerraumes*. Baden-Baden, 1967. (Translated into French as *Civilisations anciennes du Bassin méditerranéen, Corse, Sardaigne, Baléares, Les Ibères*. Paris, 1970.)

A. Arribas. *The Iberians*. London, 1963. (Spanish text, *Los Iberos*. Barcelona, 1965.)

Historia de España, dirigida por R. Menéndez Pidal:

Vol. I, 2, *España protohistórica*, 2nd ed. Madrid, 1960:
I La invasión céltica en España (M. Almagro).
II Tartessos (A. García y Bellido).
III La colonización púnica (id.).
IV La colonización griega (id.).

Vol I, 3, *España preromana*, 1st ed., Madrid, 1954.
I Los pueblos de la España céltica (J. Maluquer and B. Taracena).
II Los pueblos de la España ibérica (J. Maluquer, A. García y Bellido, J. Caro).

Primer Symposium de Prehistoria de la Península Ibérica, Pamplona, 1959. Pamplona, 1960:

Bases para el estudio de las culturas metalúrgicas de la Meseta (J. Maluquer).
Los problemas de la cultura celtibérica (F. Wattenberg).
Estado actual del conocimiento de la cultura ibérica (D. Fletcher).
El mundo ibérico (E. Cuadrado).
El impacto colonial de los pueblos semitas (M. Tarradell).

Nuevas orientaciones en el problema de Tartessos (J. Maluquer).

V Symposium Internacional de Prehistoria Peninsular Jerez de la Frontera, 1969, Tartessos y sus problemas. Barcelona, 1969.

A. Schulten. *Geografía y etnografía antiguas de la Península ibérica*, vol. 1. Madrid, 1959.

A. García y Bellido. *La Península ibérica en los comienzos de su Historia*. Madrid, 1953.

J. M. Blázquez. *Tartessos y los orígenes de la colonización fenicia en Occidente*. Salamanca, 1968.

J. Maluquer. *Tartessos*. Barcelona, 1970.

W. Schüle. *Die Meseta-Kulturen der iberischen Halbinsel*, 2 vols. Berlin, 1969.

D. Fletcher. *Problemas de la cultura ibérica*, Valencia, 1960.

Bibliography

CHAPTER 1
Iberian remains in Spanish soil

P. Paris. *Essai sur l'art et l'industrie de l'Espagne primitive*, 2 vols. Paris, 1904–1905.

P. Bosch Gimpera. *Etnología de la Península ibérica*. Barcelona, 1932.

P. Bosch Gimpera. *El poblamiento antiguo y la formación de los pueblos de España*. Mexico, 1944.

M. Gómez Moreno. 'La escritura bastuloturdetana', *Revista de Archivos, Bibliotecas y Museos (RABM)*, 69–2, 1961, pp. 879–948.

A. Tovar. *The Ancient Languages of Spain and Portugal*. New York, 1961.

J. Maluquer. *Epigrafía prelatina de la Península ibérica*. Barcelona, 1968.

P. Beltrán. *El plomo de la Bastida de les Alcuses (Mogente)*. Valencia, 1962.

E. Llobregat. *Contestania ibérica*. Valencia-Madrid, 1972.

R. Mesado. *Vinarragell*. Valencia, 1974.

CHAPTER 2
Iberia in antiquity: a legendary Far West

A. Berthelot. *Festus Avienus: Ora Maritima*. Paris, 1934.

A. Schulten. *Tartessos*. Madrid, 1945.

A. Schulten. *Fontes Hispaniae Antiquae*. I Avieno, Ora Maritima. Otros testimonios anteriores al año 500 antes de J.-C. Barcelona, 1922.

A. Schulten. *Fontes Hispaniae Antiquae*. II Del 500 antes de J.-C. hasta César. Barcelona, 1925.

A. Schulten. *Fontes Hispaniae Antiquae*. VI Estrabón. Geografía de Iberia. Barcelona, 1952.

A. García y Bellido. *Hispania Graeca*. Barcelona, 1948.

A. García y Bellido. *España y los Españoles hace dos mil años*. Madrid-Buenos Aires, 1945.

A. García y Bellido. *La España del siglo I de nuestra era según P. Mela y C. Plinio*. Madrid, 1947.

A. García y Bellido. *Fenicios y Cartagineses en Occidente*. Madrid, 1942.

H.-N. Savory. *Spain and Portugal, the prehistory of the Iberian peninsula*. London, 1968.

M. Pellicer. 'Excavaciones en la necrópolis púnica "Laurita" del Cerro de San Cristóbal (Almuñecar, Granada)', *Excavaciones arqueológicas en España 17*. Madrid, 1964.

H.-G. Niemeyer, M. Pellicer, H. Schubart. 'Altpunische Funde von der Mündung des rio Algarrobo', *Madrider Mitteilungen* 5–1964, pp. 73 ff.
M. Astruc. 'La necrópolis de Villaricos', *Informes y memorias 25 de la Comisaría general de Excavaciones arqueológicas.* Madrid, 1951.
G.-C. Picard, C. Picard. *Vie et mort de Carthage.* Paris, 1970.

CHAPTER 3
CHAPTER 4
Iberian civilisation:

Estudios de economía antigua de la Península ibérica, publicadas bajo la dirección de M. Tarradell:
Sobre el estudio económico de la España antigua (J. Caro).
Panorama económico de la primera Edad del Hierro (J. Maluquer).
Economía de la colonización fenicia (M. Tarradell).
Economía de la colonización griega (G. Trias).
Corrientes commerciales de los pueblos ibéricos (E. Cuadrado).
Instrumentos de trabajo ibéricos en la región valenciana (E. Plá).
Economía monetaria de la España antigua (A. Beltrán).
M. Ponsich, M. Tarradell. *Garum et industries antiques de salaisons.* Paris, 1965.
R. Gosse. 'Las minas y el arte minero de España en la Antigüedad', *Ampurias*, 4–1942, pp. 43–68.
J. Jaureguí, E. Poblet. 'Minería antigua en cabo de Palos,' *III Congreso arqueológico del Sudeste.* Murcia, 1947, pp. 43–68.
J. Caro. *Los pueblos de España.* Barcelona, 1946.
R. Lantier, J. Cabré. *El santuario ibérico de Castellar de Santisteban.* Madrid, 1917.
I. Calvo, J. Cabré. 'Excavaciones en la cueva y collado de los Jardines (Santa Elena, Jaén)', *Memoria de la Junta Superior de Excavaciones y Antigüedades* 8. Madrid, 1917.
J. M. Blázquez. *Religiones primitivas de España. 1, Fuentes literarias y epigráficas.* Madrid, 1962.
J. M. Blázquez. 'Dioses y caballos en el mundo ibérico', *Zephyrus*, 5–1954, pp. 193–212.
J. M. Blázquez. 'La interpretación de la pátera da Tivisa', *Ampurias*, 17–18, 1955–1956, pp. 111–140.
E. Cuadrado. 'La diosa de los caballos', *IV Congreso Internacional de Ciencias Prehistóricas, Madrid, 1954*, Saragossa, 1956, pp. 797–811.
A. García y Bellido. 'Deidades semitas en la España antigua', *Sefarad*, 24–1964, pp. 12–40; pp. 237–275.

Bibliography

A. Balil. 'Representaciones de cabezas cortadas y cabezas-trofeos en el Levante español' *IV Congreso Internacional de Ciencias Prehistóricas y Protohistóricas, Madrid 1954*, Saragossa, 1956, pp. 871–888.

G. Nicolini. 'Gestes et attitudes cultuels des figurines de bronze ibériques', *Mélanges de la Casa de Velázquez*, 4–1968, pp. 27–50.

M. Ponsich. *Implantation rurale antique sur le Bas-Guadalquivir*. Paris-Madrid, 1974.

CHAPTER 5
Towns and architecture

A. Balil. 'Casa y urbanismo en la España antigua', *Boletín del Seminario de Estudios de Arte y Arqueología*, 36–1970, pp. 289–334.

A. García y Bellido. *La arquitectura entre los Iberos*. Madrid, 1945.

A. del Castillo. 'La costa brava en la Antigüedad', *Ampurias*, 1–1939, p. 186.

M. Almagro. 'Estratigrafía de la ciudad helenístico-romana de Ampurias', *Archivo español de Arqueología* (AEArq), 20–1947, pp. 179–199.

M. Almagro. *Amporias Historia de la ciudad y guía de las excavaciones*. Barcelona 1957.

M. Oliva. 'Actividades de la Delegación provincial del Servicio Nacional de Excavaciones arqueológicas de Gerona', *Anales del Instituto de Estudios Gerundenses*, 1953–1963 (re Ullastret).

S. Vilaseca, etc. 'Excavaciones del Plan Nacional en el Castellet de Bañolas Tivisa (Tarragona)', *Informes y Memorias 20*. Madrid, 1949.

F. Pallarés, 'El poblado ibérico de San Antonio de Calaceite', *Instituto Internacional de Estudios Ligures, Colección de monografías prehistóricas y arqueológicas, 5*. Bordighera-Barcelona, 1965.

M. Tarradell. 'Ensayo de estratigrafía comparada y de cronología de los poblados ibéricos valencianos', *Saitabi*, 11–1961, p. 3.

A. Schulten. 'Meca, una ciudad rupestre ibérica', *Congreso de Arqueología del Sudeste*. Albacete, 1946, pp. 265–279.

D. Fletcher, E. Plá, J. Alcacer, 'La Bastida de les Alcuses (Mogente-Valencia)', *Serie de Trabajos Varios 14 & 25*. Valencia, 1965, 1969.

H. Schubart. 'Untersuchungen an den iberischen Befestigungen, des Montgó bei Denia (Alicante)', *Madrider Mitteilungen*, 4–1963, p. 51.

E. Diehl, P. San Martín, H. Schubart. 'Los Nietos, ein Handelsplatz des 5. bis 3. Jahrhunderts an der spanischen Levanteküste', *Madrider Mitteilungen*, 3–1962, p. 45.

H. Breuil, R. Lantier. 'El Tolmo de Minateda', *Archivo de Prehistoria Levantina*, 2–1945, pp. 213–236.

P. Paris, V. Bardaviú Ponz, R. Thouvenot. *Fouilles dans la région d'Alcañiz*, II, *Le Taratrato*. Bordeaux, 1926.

J. Cabré. *Corpus Vasorum Hispanorum, Cerámica de Azailá*. Madrid, 1944.

J. Cabré. 'Arquitectura hispánica: El sepulcro de Toya', *Archivo Español de Arte y Arqueología*, 1–1925, p. 73.

J. Cabré, F. Motos. 'La necrópolis ibérica de Tutugí (Galera, Granada)', *Memoria de la Junta Superior de Excavaciones y Antigüedades 25*, 1920.

J. Cabré, I. Calvo. 'Excavaciones de la cueva y collado de los Jardines, (Santa Elena, Jaén)', *Memoria de la Junta Superior de Excavaciones y Antigüedades 16*. Madrid, 1918.

CHAPTER 6
Sculpture: the creative genius of Iberia

D. Harden. *The Phoenicians*. London, 1962.

P. Cintas. *Manuel d'Archéologie punique*, I, 1970.

R. Lantier. *Bronzes votifs ibériques*. Paris, 1935.

G. Nicolini. *Les bronzes figurés des sanctuaires ibériques*. Paris, 1969.

G. Nicolini. 'Les bronzes votifs ibériques de la Prähistorische Staatssammlung, München', *Madrider Mitteilungen*, 7–1966, pp. 116–155.

G. Nicolini. 'A propos de l'archaïsme ibérique: une statuette inédite de la collection Le Corneur', *Mélanges de la Casa de Velázquez*, 3, 1967, pp. 501–502.

G. Nicolini. 'Les bronzes ibériques', *Objets*, 4–5, pp. 65–81.

F. Álvarez Ossorio. *Catálogo de los exvotos de bronce ibéricos*, Museo arqueológico nacional. Madrid, 1941.

H. Sandars. 'Pre-Roman bronze offerings from Despeñaperros', *Archaeologia*, 1906, pp. 69–92.

A. Arribas. 'En torno al arte ibérico, Catálogo de la colección de exvotos ibéricos Richard de Bruselas', *Homenaje al Conde de la Vega del Sella*. Oviedo, 1956. pp. 255–278.

E. Kukahn. 'Estatuilla de bronce de un guerrero a caballo del poblado ibérico de La Bastida de les Alcuses (Mogente, Valencia)', *Archivo de Prehistoria Levantina*, V, 1954, pp. 147–158.

M. Almagro. 'L'influence grecque sur le monde ibérique', *Actes du VIIIe congrès international d'Archéologie classique, Paris, 1963*. Paris, 1965, pp. 87–93.

A. García y Bellido. 'Un "Apolo" arcaico de bronce', *IPEK*, 1932–1933, p. 103.

Bibliography

A. García y Bellido. 'Algunos problemas de arte y cronología ibéricas', *Archivo Español de Arqueología*, 50–1943, pp. 78–108.

A. García y Bellido. *La Dama de Elche y el conjunto de piezas arqueológicas reingresadas en España en 1941*. Madrid, 1943.

A. García y Bellido. *Ars Hispaniae, I, Arte ibérico*, p. 219.

P. Paris. *Essai sur l'art et l'industrie de l'Espagne primitive*, I, 1903, II, 1904.

R. Carpenter. *The Greeks in Spain*. Bryn Mawr, 1925.

E. Cuadrado. 'Excavaciones en el santuario ibérico del Cigarralejo (Mula, Murcia)', *Informes y Memorias de la Comisaría general de Excavaciones arqueológicas*, 21. Madrid, 1950.

A. Fernández de Avilés. 'Esculturas del Cerro de Los Santos, La colección Velasco', *Archivo Español de Arqueología*, 53–1943, pp. 361–387.

A. Fernández de Avilés. 'Cerro de Los Santos', *Excavaciones arqueológicas en España*, 55. Madrid, 1966.

J. A. Gaya Nuño. *Escultura ibérica*. Madrid, 1964.

A. Engel, P. Paris. 'Une forteresse ibérique à Osuna', *Nouvelles archives des missions scientifiques*, 13–1906, p. 404.

CHAPTER 7
Iberian painted pottery

J. de Mata Carriazo. 'El tesoro y las primeras excavaciones en "El Carambolo" (Camas, Sevilla)', *Excavaciones arqueológicas en España*, 68. Madrid, 1970.

M. Pellicer, W. Shüle. 'El Cerro del Real, Galera (Granada)', *Excavaciones arqueológicas en España*, 12. Madrid, 1962.

M. Pellicer. 'Las primitivas cerámicas a torno pintadas hispanas', *Archivo Español Arqueología*, 41–1968, pp. 60–90.

M. Pellicer. 'El Tossal de les Tenalles de Sidamunt y sus cerámicas pintadas', *Archivo Español de Arqueología*, 39–1966, pp. 97–112.

H. Niemeyer, H. Schubart. *Toscanos, 1964*. Berlin, 1969.

D. Fletcher. *La necrópolis de la Solivella, Alcalá de Chivert (Castellón)*. Valencia, 1965.

M. Almagro. *La necrópolis de Ampurias*. Barcelona, I, 1953, II, 1955.

E. Cuadrado. 'El momento actual de la cerámica de barniz rojo', *VI° Congreso Nacional de Arqueología*. Oviedo, 1959.

C. Aranegui. 'Cerámica gris de los poblados ibéricos valencianos', *Papeles del Laboratorio de Arqueología de Valencia*, 6–1969, pp. 113–131.

I. Ballester, D. Fletcher, E. Plá, F. Jorda, J. Alcacer. *Corpus Vasorum Hispanorum, Cerámica de San Miguel, Liria*. Madrid, 1954.

G. Nieto. 'La necrópolis hispánica del Cabecico del Tesoro, Verdolay (Murcia)', *Boletín del Seminario de Estudios de Arte y Arqueología, Universidad de Valladolid*, 6–1939–40, pp. 137–160; 9–1942–3, pp. 191–196; 10–1943–5, pp. 165–175.

A. García y Bellido. 'Nuevos datos sobre la cronología final de la cerámica ibérica y sobre su extensión extrapeninsular', *Archivo Español de Arqueología*, 25–1952, pp. 39–45.

A. García y Bellido, 'Estado actual del problema referente a la expansión de la cerámica ibérica por la cuenca occidental del Mediterráneo', *Archivo Español de Arqueología*, 30 1957, pp. 90–106.

A. García y Bellido. 'La pintura mayor entre los Iberos', *Archivo Español de Arqueología*, 18–1945, pp. 250–257.

A. Ramos. *Excavaciones en La Alcudia (Elche)*. Valencia, 1970.

S. Nordstrom. *La céramique ibérique peinte de la région d'Alicante*. Stockholm, 1973.

CHAPTER 8
Metalwork
and jewellery

G. Becatti. *Oreficerie antiche dalle minoiche alle barbariche*. Rome, 1955.

A. Blanco. 'Orientalia. Estudios de objetos fenicios y orientalizantes en la península'. *Archivo Español de Arqueología*, 29–1956, pp. 3–51.

A. Blanco. 'Orientalia II', *Archivo Español de Arqueología*, 33–1960, pp. 3–43.

E. Kukahn, A. Blanco. 'El Tesoro de "El Carambolo" ', *Archivo Español de Arqueología*, 32–1959, pp. 38–49.

J. de Mata Carriazo. 'El Tesoro y las primeras Excavaciones de Ébora (Sanlúcar de Barrameda)', *Excavaciones arqueológicas en España*, *69*. Madrid, 1970.

J. M. Blázquez. 'Joyas orientalizantes extremeñas del Museo Arqueológico Nacional', *Zephyrus*, 14–1963, pp. 5–15.

K. Raddatz. *Die Schatzfunde der Iberischen Halbinsel vom Ende des 3. bis zur Mitte des 1. Jahrhunderts vor Christi Geburt*. Berlin, 1970.

J. Maluquer. 'Un interesante lote de bronces, hallados en el castro de Sanchorreja (Ávila)', *Zephyrus*, 7–1957, pp. 241–256.

J. Cabré. 'Decoraciones hispánicas', *Archivo Español de Arte y Arqueología*, 13–1937, p. 93.

H. Sandars. 'The Weapons of the Iberians', *Archaeologia*, 64–1913, pp. 1–105.

J. and M. E. Carré. 'La caetra y el scutum en Hispania durante la segunda Edad del Hierro', *Boletín del Seminario de Estudios de Arte y Arqueología, Universidad de Valladolid*, 1939 1940, pp. 57–84.

G. Bonsor. 'Les colonies préromaines dans la vallée du Bétis', *Revue Archéologique*, 35–1899.

E. Cuadrado. 'La fíbula anular hispánica y sus problemas', *Zephyrus*, 8–1957, p. 5.

E. Cuadrado. 'Los recipientes rituales metálicos llamados braserillos púnicos', *Archivo Español de Arqueología*, 29–1956, pp. 52–84.

A. García y Bellido. 'Nuevos jarros de bronce tartessios', *Archivo Español de Arqueología*, 37–1964, pp. 50–80.

J. de Mata. *Carriazo Tartessos y el Carambolo*. Madrid, 1973.

Index

Index

Index